OUR MEMOIR COLLECTION

EVERYBODY HAS A STORY

By
**Campbell Community Center
Memoir Class Writers**

Compiled and Edited by
Dr. Roger Hite
and
gael (Mustapha) Doyle-Oroyan, Instructor

"Every life is a treasure chest of timeless tales."

---Madge Walls

Second Printing

Acknowledgements

Special thanks to:

gael Doyle-Oroyan, instructor, has taught classes for more than four decades in Hawaii, Arizona, Washington, and Oregon. These stories by her students are presented to inspire and encourage others to record their memoirs for family, friends, and future generations.

Dr. Roger Hite, compiling editor and publisher with his great ability to use print on demand to produce this book.

Participating students for their hard work in developing and finalizing these wonderful, memorable, and readable stories.

Celeste Campbell Community Center for offering this class that helps individuals tell their life stories and especially Tom Powers, program supervisor, and his very competent, helpful staff.

Foreword

Our memoir writing classes at Campbell Community Center in Eugene, OR offer opportunities to produce a variety of incredible and inspiring personal stories from senior citizens who have lived through the historical, changing times of the 20th and 21st centuries to date. Their tales share sage, salty, witty, serious, and tragic experiences related to a variety of values, education, life, love, liberty, and wisdom.

I believe every person has a story to tell about their life. I am pleased that through my facilitation many students continue to remain in class-after-class as they move forward to record their remarkable life stories for family, friends, and future generations.

I share my students' hope that this collection of some of their encounters with life will encourage and inspire others to pick up pen and paper or go to their computers to start recording their own stories.

gael Doyle-Oroyan,
Instructor
May 2013

Table of Contents

(Chapters Titled With Each Contributing Author's Name)

Memoirs

Memoirs are a lot like people.
Never are two just alike.
Some are funny, some are sunny
Some, keep us awake at night.

There are those that set you dreaming
Of the places they describe.
Some, are pleasantly surprising
Some, require a better scribe.

They hold a mirror to the outlook
and the writer's inner thoughts.
Revealing, oftentimes, their darkest
Wounds, more than they perhaps, ought.

But memories are best when shared,
With our friends or family.
Written memoirs make them all
Available more easily.

Enjoy the triumph with the writers,
Of both the painful and the fun.
Now, relax with us and share them.
Thank God they are finally done.

--David Mckee

1

"Westward Ho! To Chicuala-*what?*"

By
Vicki Bunnett

[EDITOR'S NOTE: *Vicki Bunnett was born in North Dakota and after a brief and undistinguished stint at the University of North Dakota left to live in Los Angeles, Scotland, Washington State, San Francisco, Zimbabwe, San Francisco, and Los Angeles. Many adventures in love, life, work, and additional brief forays into education ensued. She is now retired and living in Eugene, Oregon.]*

* * *

We were up early and on the road to Chokwe, a farming community on the Limpopo River in southern Mozambique. With a population of 67,000, Chokwe, a cross between a city and a shantytown, put me in mind of a river flooding its banks, sprawling and organic, expanding into the surrounding fields. Two years later, Chokwe would attain a sad notoriety when Cyclone Eline devastated the region, sweeping away a huge bridge in Xai-Xai, displacing hundreds of thousands of people and leaving the world with the indelible image of a marooned woman giving birth in a tree above raging floodwaters as rescue helicopters arrive. But this early morning, all was calm and bright.

In Chokwe, we picked up some fruit and bread for breakfast and Dave, the Aussie driver, went off to gather information about the road we planned to take to the Zimbabwean border post of Chicualacuala. On the road south from Vilankulo we had asked for advice at each stop about the best route back to Zimbabwe. Everyone mentioned the road to Chicualacuala but opinions about road conditions varied wildly from okay to impassable. The last person we spoke to in Chokwe expressed enthusiasm saying he had a friend who knew a man who had come that way recently, so driven by our non-existent alternatives given that this was the only route for our group of five ex-pats (one man and four women) to return to Zimbabwe from our Easter holiday, we decided to give it a try.

It's funny how roads drawn in a firm black line on a map give an impression of solid engineering and safety, especially when the traveler desperately needs the road to be passable. True, we saw virtually no towns or villages on the map but we decided that wouldn't be a problem after we carefully calculated the mileage and filled up both the tank on the SUV and the extra jerry cans that

Dave had brought. Full of totally unwarranted optimism and with a somewhat uneasy sense of adventure, we started west at around 7 a.m.

The road out of Chokwe was not a road so much as a series of bottomless potholes connected by small ribbons of asphalt. After an hour wasted traveling a couple of painfully slow miles, we followed the lead of the locals and drove off the road and into the ditches; rutted as they were, they were better than the road. Judging by the number of tire tracks we were fairly certain land mines weren't a problem here.

When the "paved" road ended, a gravel road in good condition continued west. The gravel eventually became thick sand, slowed us down considerably. The day grew hotter. We met no other vehicles and no one traveling in our direction. We saw nothing but an occasional distant building smashed by artillery or pocked by gunfire from the recently-ended civil war, a reminder not to stray from the road when we stopped.

Twice, trains on the tracks paralleling the road slowly gained on us, trundled alongside and then left us behind, the young soldiers they carried laughing and pointing at us and waving us back in the direction from which we had come, a somewhat disconcerting warning. The road was broken at regular intervals by concrete abutments off to each side that funneled water through troughs to metal grates over the roadway – not really bridges, but clearly meant to facilitate passage over water. The further we drove, the closer the intervals where water crossed the road became. We didn't realize until later that the road crossed and recrossed a river which owed its size to how much rain had fallen recently.

We stopped a couple of times when nature called and once to add the reserve fuel to the tank. Five hours after our departure from Chokwe, we had slowed to around thirty miles per hour because of increasingly wet road conditions, but were still confident, assuming that we had sufficient resources for whatever might arise. The heat was now suffocating and the humidity made our clothes feel like damp towels as we had decided not to use the AC to conserve fuel. The nausea I felt from malaria drugs worsened as the SUV slid crazily over the damp, sandy ruts of the road. The area became swampier with large, dense trees along the sides of the now serpentine road. Then, as we came around a large curve, we saw that for the next quarter of a mile, the road was covered by a lake - quite a well-established looking lake, with lily pads, water birds and gentle ripples. The real deal. Sunlight shimmered on the water and in the distance we could just see the road as it emerged from the lake through some reeds.

At this point, we were closer to the border than we were to Chokwe. We had used more than half our fuel. We were no longer anywhere near the railroad, not that that would have made any difference. Our cell phones were out of range of any tower on the planet. In the SUV, as we sat staring at the water, silence reigned.

Dave switched the vehicle off and we got out. All four females suddenly felt the need to pee again even though we had just gone. Dave probably did too, but managed to maintain his stoic, macho persona. As we filed in turn to the rear of the SUV, Dave took off his socks and waded into the water in his sandals. Returning to the front of the vehicle we stood at the water's edge and watched his receding back as he made his tentative way further into the water. It appeared that the water came no higher than his knees, but we couldn't be sure the SUV would make it until he was all the way across. He walked from side to side, testing the width of the road with a stick, making sure of the bottom and finally reached the other side. He waved in an encouraging way and started back. When he arrived, he reported that the road felt solid enough to cross. There was a small submerged wooden bridge near the other side that he would have to approach carefully, but no other hazards that he could see. Amid high-fives, huge sighs of relief and congratulations we decided to take a short break, have a bite, and then cross the water. Dave would drive and we women would walk behind.

We snacked and though it may sound imprudent we each had one of the best cold beers I've ever had in my life. Then while Dave checked all the luggage and equipment to make sure nothing would shift, we rolled up our pants and hitched up our skirts or put on shorts and decided which shoes or sandals to sacrifice. Dave got back in the Pajaro and turned the key. Silence. He tried again. Nothing. After a long pause, he put his head down on the steering wheel and tried one more time. Nada. We crowded around anxiously. Oddly, that did nothing for the Pajaro and even less for Dave's mood. He popped the hood, got out and propping it open, peered at the engine, fiddled with various bits and then tried the starter again. Nothing. Quietly but with great sincerity and depth of feeling, he spoke a stream of expletives as colorful and inventive as you would expect from a man who had spent considerable time over the years driving around the Australian outback in the company of other large, manly blokes. Since he was eloquently expressing what we all were feeling, no one even blinked.

Then he remembered that he had had the anti-theft immobilizer looked at a few weeks prior for an intermittent problem. The mechanic hadn't been able to find anything and Dave had had no further problems – until now. He thought if he could disable the immobilizer, he might be able to get the vehicle started. After a tense quarter hour under the hood, he dispiritedly reported that he wasn't sure he could safely disarm the device without creating more problems. Disgusted, he climbed back into the Pajaro, turned the key and amazingly, the engine sprang to life. We all looked at each other in astonished joy and cheered.

Dave yelled that he was starting across. He advanced slowly into the water, and as elated as we all felt, we followed the SUV with a certain trepidation fueled by fears of bilharzia, water snakes, quicksand, landmines, crocodiles and hippos, none of which were far-fetched. Once safely on the other side, we climbed gratefully into the Pajaro, and after navigating several additional but less impressive stretches of water, the road started climbing and eventually we resumed normal speed on a reassuringly dry road.

We soon drove through the single town on the map, consisting of a vacant, vaguely municipal looking building, a couple of thatched huts, no people and no fuel stations. A couple of uneventful hours later, we reached the border post at Chicualacuala. The gate was shut and locked with only a small boy in attendance, this being a holiday. We paid a small tip for him to run and get the border agent, who was furious at being called to duty on his day off. But after appraising our potential for grateful generosity, he grudgingly proceeded with his bureaucratic duties

He required all of us regardless of nationality to complete the long-form visa application which was very long indeed, and informed us that the maximum entry fee would be required and we understood that a generous gratuity would be as well. Then, after changing the date on his official stamp, with a grand flourish, he stamped our passports. What he forgot to change was the year, demonstrating that no one had been through this deserted border post since the previous year.

This particular entry point necessitated traveling through a Zimbabwean national game park called Gonarezhou, famous for its large elephant population. What the guidebooks don't say is that during both the Zimbabwe Independence War and the Mozambican Civil War, the park was heavily land-mined and many animals, particularly elephants were killed by mines or poached for ivory by combatants on all sides. As a result, the elephants are understandably aggressive toward humans.

Ignorance being what it is, we blissfully drove into the park and within a quarter of a mile, a large bull elephant stepped out of the trees and paced slowly into the road in front of the SUV. Excitedly, we grabbed our cameras and hung out of opened doors to take pictures as the elephant pawed the road and flapped his ears. Dave warned that we should be ready to leave quickly because the big male was showing signs of aggression. At that, the elephant abruptly began to charge towards us. Dave yelled and we slammed the doors, dropping our cameras and screaming. Often the initial charge is false but as we got up to 45 miles per hours in reverse, the elephant was still coming and didn't have the look like an animal that was just testing our resolve.

As terror was turning into total panic, two park rangers in a jeep sped around us from behind and went straight at the elephant which pulled up short and seemed to rethink his plan to trample us into the ground. After chasing the elephant back into the trees, the rangers returned and kindly escorted us through the rest of the park to the exit.

Approaching our hotel for the night, and finally able to laugh shakily at our narrow escapes we were given the bird, so to speak, for a final time that day: a startled guinea fowl, a singularly stupid representative of the bird world, flew up from the bush and into the windshield, cracking it from top to bottom and after being hurled to the roadside, bumbled off, clucking indignantly, into the bush.

* * *

"That Gang That Sang"

We sang together, gathered around the piano while my mother, Shirley, played. My mother and the three oldest kids sang harmonies and the youngest three carried the soprano line in their sweet, high voices; but we switched these roles depending on the song and which of the boys was going through puberty. We sang Heart of my Heart, Sentimental Journey, Blues in the Night and Far Away Places. When relatives visited from out of town to stay with my rich aunt, Cleo, we were always asked over to the house to sing. Cleo's favorites were a rollicking This Old House and the Tennessee Waltz. When I stayed with Cleo as a child I refused to go to sleep until we sang Mockingbird Hill at least three times. We sang carols at

Christmas and made up a large contingent in the church choir. My father and his parents sang too, the men with their special songs. My father, Archie, sang Goodnight Irene and I'll Be Seeing You in a fine strong tenor. My grandfather, Ed, always sang Bye Bye Blackbird, slow and lonesome. My grandparents sang My Gal Sal and Me and My Gal together and Grandma Adeline played her "accordeen" and everyone joined in on the choruses.

Sometimes when my mother sat down at the piano, we could tell by what she played like Rhapsody in Blue or Red Roses for a Blue Lady that she didn't want a sing-along. Those times, we'd find a corner nearby and listen quietly. But if she sat down and started into Oklahoma! we all came running. On summer evenings, if nobody wanted to sing, I went outside and climbed one of the big trees in the yard, and from my perch sang until darkness fell and the lights in the living room drew me back in to join the family watching Ed Sullivan. As we grew older and my mother played the piano less, my younger sister, Paula, and I took up the slack. Every night when we did the dishes, after arguing about who would wash and who would dry, we'd argue about what song to sing, who would sing what part and what the words to Tallahassee Lassie or Norwegian Wood were. Between arguments we sang. My mother often came and slammed the kitchen door shut so the rest of the family could hear the TV.

We always sang on road trips. Coming home from my grandparents' cabin at Island Lake in Minnesota, we sang as we drove by the farms and roadhouses, through the woods and fields and finally over the Old Point Bridge, a rickety one-lane wooden structure over the Red River between East Grand Forks and Grand Forks. My brother and I sang as we sat in the car in a dark alley behind Whitey's Bar in East Grand Forks, waiting for my dad who went in to have just one drink and came out hours later in no fit condition to drive. My brother and I later sang together in a talent show at the University of North Dakota and won the "People's Favorite" award by pretending to be Sonny and Cher for our few moments of fame.

I grew up thinking all families sang together and was surprised to learn they didn't. When I left home at 18, the world seemed sadly quiet and I did my best to fill it up singing by myself, but it wasn't the same. Nevertheless, I sang my way through my own, solitary road trips and those with my husband when I married. We sang on trips: Goodnight Irene in a Scottish bar and Dancing Cheek to Cheek in a Florence, Italy trattoria.

In my 60's, I developed vocal tremor and self-consciousness has silenced me. Death took my parents and three of my siblings too soon. I would love to have my voice back, and would give anything "if once more I could listen to that gang that sang **Heart of my Heart.**"

2

"New York City Public Library On Fifth Avenue"

By
Joel Cherrytree

[EDITOR'S NOTE: *Joel Cherrytree, 75, is a retired school counselor who worked in Springfield public schools for 18 years. Today he is an active tennis player, swimmer, hiker and lover of the outdoors. He enjoys an intellectual life through book clubs, reading Catholic theologians, traveling and being with his wife and two daughters.*]

* * *

Last year, I visited my daughter in New York City.

As we were walking on Fifth Avenue, we passed the New York City Public Library with its two celebrated stone lions at its entrance. Jenny unexpectedly asked me *"Have you ever been in that library?"*

I hesitated for a moment, recalling an experience of 50 years ago and I said, *"Yes, I have been in that library."* I told her this story.

In 1956, I was an 18 year old freshman at Fairfield University, A Jesuit College, in Fairfield, Connecticut.

During the Christmas vacation, I came home to Queens, a borough of New York City, with a major task to complete my first college term paper.

After 50 years, I still remember the topic of the paper: "The Historical Roots of Sacraments." I had no idea that this topic would be so difficult to research.

Because the topic of this paper was so esoteric, I could not find any books on this question in the local library in Queens.

I decided to go to the main library in Manhattan on 42nd street to find books on my topic.

On a snowy winter day, I left for the library taking a bus from home to the subway for a long trip into Manhattan. The City was magically covered with a blanket of whiteness. In my mind, I was not traveling to the library, but I was a wandering scholar riding on my horse from University of Paris to Heidelberg University.

After a two hour trip, I walked past the celebrated lions and into the main reading room of the library; I was awed.

The main reading room was like a cathedral, with high ceilings reaching 60 feet tall, filled with hundreds of separate desks each with its own reading lamp. Each person had their own desk piled with books.

I was immediately informed by the librarian about their strict rules.

I had to find my books in the card catalogue. Then I had to write the name of the book with its number on a file card and give this information to the librarian. After that process, she would find the book. No computer to help me!

These books could not be taken home, but had to be kept on your own private desk to be used the next day.

I had to return each day for a week to the library to complete my paper. Since this library was a famous research library, I discovered this library had too many books on my topic.

After a long selecting process, I discovered five books relevant to my topic.

But these books were not for a freshman college student taking a beginning course who never read a dense, scholarly book in my life. These tomes were for graduate students. But I was stuck. These advanced, scholarly books were all I had. So I struggled to read and understand these books, took my notes, organized them and listed my sources in my bibliography.

Before long, I was lost in the wilderness. How do I begin the paper? How would I write this paper? No one taught me how to begin a paper, organize it, and then to write it. I had no friends who could help me.

Returning to Fairfield, I was proud and hopeful of my completed paper. As I entered my dorm room, I met my roommate Marty who was worried and upset because he had not written his paper. Marty went directly to our college library, found a book on his topic, and copied word-for-word from the book and typed up his paper and submitted it the next day.

A week later our papers were returned. As the Jesuit called our names, the students walked dramatically to his desk and collected their papers and their grades. When he called my name I walked nervously to him. He looked at me sternly and said, *"I lowered your grade because the books listed in your bibliography you could never have found or read."*

I tried to explain that I got these books at the New York City Public Library. The Jesuit shook his head in disbelief.

When I returned to my room, Marty was smiling. He received an "A" grade for his plagiarized paper with many positive comments about his scholarship.

Jenny said, *"What a jerk! Were you upset, Dad?"*

But coming back to the moment, *"Jenny, I have very good memories of this hard-won achievement without any negative feelings."*

But the story continues. When I applied for a very competitive counseling position in Springfield, Oregon, I had to write about a personal experience relating to my own education. I wrote about this week of researching at the New York City Public Library. The personnel director said he appreciated this essay and I got the job.

I might have gotten an undeserved poor grade from this unappreciated Jesuit, but the memory of my moment of courage will always be there for me as I face the next challenge of life.

3

"The Wedding"

By
Dave McKee

[EDITOR'S NOTE: Dave McKee grew up on Poodle Creek, near Noti, Oregon. He and his wife, Doris now live in Coburg, Oregon and are both active in volunteer work as well as operate their Real Estate investment business. They have eight children, 22 grandchildren and 28 great grandchildren. Dave is a charter member of the Oregon Tuba Association Ensemble, now in its 34th year. He is a graduate of Elmira High school and is a member of the Lane County Republican Party. Dave's hobbies are writing poetry and playing his tuba for hospice care patients. He is a member of Eugene Faith Center.]

* * *

Funny, how events sometimes unfold in ways we never expect. When Doris and I married, it was not really the event we had in mind.

Let me explain.

Doris and I had dated for about two years. She had two daughters, Dawn 12 and Cheri 16 and I had four sons.

Randy 13, Glenn 14, Mike 16 & Bill 18 and two daughters. Patty 10 and Colleen 17. My daughters lived in Alaska with their mother.

Colleen had dated a young man in Anchorage for a year or more, when her mother decided to move to Roswell, New Mexico. Absence makes the heart grow fonder, they say. It worked that way with Colleen and her beaux, Darrell. Soon after she moved, he called and asked her to marry him. He was 20. She told him he needed to get my permission, so he called and we had the usual conversation. A good young man, he always treated her with respect and was a good carpenter. I gave my consent and he flew down to Roswell to marry her. Colleen sent out wedding invitations and did all the usual preparations. Meanwhile, my two youngest sons were visiting their mother in Roswell, so I made plans to drive a car there for the wedding, and then give the car to the kids, so they could drive it home to Alaska, having a honeymoon along the way. Sounded so romantic!

Meanwhile, Colleen's mother had to fly back to Alaska to sign some legal papers and while there, she and Darrell's mother decided that, since all the kids' friends lived in Alaska, they should have the wedding there. I got a call from Colleen the next day, sounding upset with her mother, Darrell was upset by the expense of losing two weeks work and still not getting married and Colleen felt upset about having to cancel all those wedding invitations. My boys were ready to come home anyway, so I proposed that we put them all on a flight to Eugene, get the kids married here and send them to Alaska with the car I planned to give them. Sounded like a plan.

When the kids got here, we called the Lane County Court-house to get a marriage license. They asked the ages of the kids. Darrell had to be 21 in Oregon or have parental consent. Well, I reasoned, Idaho allows marriage at eighteen, let's take them there. So, the next day we loaded Colleen, Darrell and Colleen's cousin Robin in the kid's car; Doris and I and Bill in our car, and took off for Payette, Idaho. Colleen had sewn her own wedding dress, a beautiful creation in white satin. Bill would start football practice at Whitman college the following Monday, so after the wedding he would catch a bus for school and Doris and I would bring Robin back to Eugene with us.

All went well until we arrived in Payette. The court house was an old stone building, with broken concrete front steps and one side tilted away. There was a central hallway with a window to the clerk's office to do business through. Colleen's face just fell when she saw this dismal building. When we knocked on the window, the clerk said "we close at 5:00 p.m., sorry."

"We looked at our watches 4:10 pm......We had forgotten that Payette is on Mountain Time! So, we rented a motel room for the girls and one for the boys. Colleen was still disappointed at the prospect of being married in that crummy courthouse, so I decided to call around to see if a local pastor would marry them in his church. I found one very agreeable, so we made plans to do that as soon as they had their license. The pastor asked their ages, and when told Darrell was 20, said "Idaho just changed their law to require parental consent until age 21 one for the man.

Now we were all upset.

In my usual brilliance, I suggested, "Well anyone 18 can get married in Nevada. Let's go to Winnemucca, It's about a five hour drive from here and you can get married and I'm giving you this car. You can drive to Alaska, and decide if you want to tell your mothers about already being married."

Bill said, "I have to be at the college, I'm getting off here." So Colleen, Darrell, Robin, Doris and I headed for Winnemucca.

We arrived about 4:00 p.m. and headed to the courthouse. This one was an old but impressive stone building with a spacious clerk's office. We took a seat on a long bench in the waiting area and saw a procession of marriage license applicants work their way to the clerk's desk. The couple just ahead of us were both 20. The young man's mother said, "I'll sign for him."

Darrel's face fell a mile. It seems that Nevada had also changed their law to 21 for the man or consent of a parent. Now what do we do?

Over dinner at a local casino, we came up with a solution. Robin, I said, how would you like to go to Alaska? Darrell and Colleen, take this car and this money and you three drive to Alaska, have the wedding and I'll send for Robin.

As they disappeared from sight, Doris and I looked at each other. What do we do now? We had decided that at some point we would get married, but Cheri had stuck her head in the car window as we were leaving and said, "Now don't you two get married. I want to be there whenever you do."

We had planned to pick up Doris's youngest, Dawn from her grandparent's in Redwood City, so we reasoned; we would get married in Carson City, then take our time driving to get Dawn, not telling her we were married; then we'd drive home and go back to our respective homes and announce our wedding plans so the kids could plan it as they had wanted to. The first step was to get the license and a ring. The hard part was the emotional barrier. Both of us had had a bad first marriage. The thought of making a second mistake was daunting. As we drove into a shopping mall to look for a wedding band, Doris got so sick she upchucked in the parking lot.

We managed to gather ourselves enough to get the paper work and a ring, then rented a motel and began calling around to find a church that would marry us. Doris just could not go to a marriage chapel/tattoo parlor or whatever. After several calls, I found a LDS church that answered their phone. "Sure," he said. "We are having a board meeting, but as soon as we finish, we'll do it for you."

Doris and I met with the elder in his study. He gave us a little booklet titled, "don't let the sun go down on your anger," a book of good advice to married couples, about communication and commitment. We were married there with a couple from their church as witnesses. Then, off to pick up Dawn in Redwood City with a stop in Lake Tahoe, where we stayed at Harvey's casino and hotel. We had a beautiful view of the lake from our room and a nice, relaxed time.

Dawn had always viewed me guardedly. She had been traumatized by her father in many ways, although she loved him. Perhaps she couldn't quite let herself like me, without feeling guilty about betraying her father. In any case, we told Doris' parents about our wedding, but not Dawn. My brother lived in San Jose, not far away, so we drove there to spend a night and visit. They thought it a blast that we had married. About 6:00 pm that evening, I had a call from Alaska. It seemed that, because I was Colleen's legal guardian, she had to have my permission to get married! I had to go to the nearest telegraph office to wire my permission before she could proceed with her wedding.

The trip home with Dawn was war. She planted herself between Doris and I, and with her arms folded and a scowl on her face, made it clear that she wasn't happy about me being around her mom. About ten miles out, we tried to be diplomatic by saying "what would you think about it if we decided to get married some day?"

EXPLOSION! No, no no. Shaking her head and sobbing, Dawn was not in any mood to talk about that idea at all. Doris and I looked at each other. "What have we done?" we telegraphed. Dawn brooded for another ten miles or so, and then said, "I guess that would mean I wouldn't see my grandma and grandpa ever again."

"No sweetheart," we said, "they would still be your grandparents, and you could see them just like always."

"Well I won't see my friends anymore."

"Yes you will. You won't even change schools," we said.

"Oh," she said.

Then, as we passed a billboard that announced the Nut Tree restaurant and amusement park coming up, she said "I don't suppose we could stop there could we?"

"Sure," I said. "Let's have lunch there."

Her dad would never stop there, but would drive on by. A smile started to show a little. After a nice lunch and a little shopping, we got back in the car. This time Dawn headed for the back seat and was happy as could be all the way home. When we arrived, we went to our separate homes, called a local pastor that we both knew and made arrangements for a wedding, telling him that we already were married. He asked to see the license, and laughed as we told him of our little deception. Cheri planned the whole ceremony, sent out the invitations, and organized the event. Randy insisted on riding his bicycle to the wedding and, of course, had a breakdown on the way. Arriving with grease on his shirt. But all in all, a memorable occasion.

The final chapter came almost two years later. Doris mentioned that our anniversary was coming up in August. Cheri said, 'No mom, your anniversary is in September.''

"Well Cheri," Doris said, "I hate to tell you this, but we were married the same time as Colleen. in August."

Cheri said with feigned anger "You mean you let me do all that, and you were already married? Oh well, it was fun anyway."

P.S. This year, we celebrate our 42nd anniversary.

* * *

"My Day"

I used to daydream about going to Bible School or Bible College, not a real plan you know, just a vague "maybe someday, if it works out" kind of an idea. What a surprise when I found that it turned into a reality. I'm actually here! But my daydream did not include how going to college would affect my everyday life. I thought I'd just be a full-time, pre-paid student while my wife supported me by taking in washing or something. I'd spend my days in the library pursuing obscure writings on exotic themes or in classrooms, astounding the faculty with my great wisdom—everything done decently and in order. But after three weeks of college life, all I can say is that my major seems to be time juggling.

My typical week goes something like this: On Monday Theology class starts at 8:20 a.m. My last class ends at 12:05 p.m. Then I have to make a decision. Do I go to Goshen and work on a man's bathroom I dismantled two weeks ago, or go work on the counseling center I was supposed to start on last week, or maybe the house I started to paint but haven't finished over on Monroe Street? I check out four theology books and decide to work on the Goshen job until 6:00 p.m. After supper I have to decide whether I dare go to tuba ensemble practice or to the library. I decide on the library and do research until 9:00 p.m.

Tuesday begins with New Testament Survey at 7:30 a.m. Writing Skills class ends at 11:10 a.m. When I get home I find a note from my wife: "The lady from Monroe St. wants to know why you haven't been painting her house?

I call and tell her "I'll be there tomorrow for sure."

I find another note: "Dick Morisette wants you to stop by tomorrow morning for prayer time at 8:30 a.m." Also Don Anderson called to tell you "the inspector gave us the go-ahead so we can start the insulation now." I decide to work at Goshen until 6:00 pm. After supper I grab my theology books to read. At 10:00 p.m I realize that I haven't done my Early Church History assignment due tomorrow. I finish my assignment at 1:00 a.m..

The first class on Wednesday is Early Church History at 9:20 am. I leave early so that I can stop by the school to have a prayer time with Dick. Then I go on to class with the last one ending at 12:05 p.m. It's raining so I go home, change clothes and call the lady at Monroe Street to tell her I can't paint today. She isn't home so I decide to go to the library. On the way up the hill the sun comes out. I go ahead but feel guilty and spend half my time trying to think of a good explanation to give her. I write a report on a magazine article for Spiritual Growth class due Thursday on "Prayer", Then I discover it should have on "Authority", so I write another one, this time on

"Authority". When I got home the lady had called and wants me to call her back---forget it! I go to prayer meeting, returning at 9:00 p.m. I decide to get started on those theology books. So I sit down and read for ten minutes and fall asleep.

On Thursday, New Testament Survey starts at 7:30 a.m. Spiritual Growth class ends at 11:10 a.m. I find out it doesn't matter what subject my report is on for Spiritual Growth. I have special prayer for my attitude. Then I decide to go to the lady's house to paint. It starts to rain, but I go anyway. When I drive in she comes out of the house, so I get out of the pick-up to face the music. She says, "I called to tell you I think I want to change the color" (what is an English word meaning both relief and despair)? I send a quick "Oh-Lord-anoint-these words" prayer and talk her out of it. Afterward I pray for my attitude….again! I paint until 5:00 p.m. and go home for supper. My wife says, "The man from Goshen called to see why you haven't been there for two days?" After supper I work on my Early Church History assignment until midnight.

Biblical Theology starts at 8:25 a.m on Friday and Bible Study Methods ends at 12:05 pm. I go by the counseling center but I have forgotten the key, so I go home, eat lunch, and go to Goshen to work on the bathrooms instead. I had to promise him I would work Saturday too. At 5:00 p.m. I go home and my wife gives me a message from Don to "call him" and one from a tenant who has a mouse in her kitchen. While I'm eating, the lady calls to see if I will be there Saturday to paint. The tuba ensemble leader calls to see if I can play next Saturday at 1:00 p.m. They need a third chair desperately, and questioned why I didn't show up on Monday. After supper I go to the tenant's place and set a mouse trap. Then I come home and read theology books until 11:30 p.m.

On Saturday I leave the house at 8:30 a.m. to go to Goshen. I work until noon then go to Monroe Street and paint until 5:00 p.m., go to the library until 9:00p.m., and finish my Early Church History assignment. When I turn in the driveway at home, my wife comes out of the house to tell me the tenant's cat stepped in the mouse trap and ran under the house. So I take the flashlight over and crawl under the porch and take the trap off the dumb cat!! The tenant isn't supposed to have a cat in the first place. Now they are mad about their cat. So am I, so I offer to haul the cat or the mouse trap away. They say, "Ok, we'll keep the trap."

"Now what do I do with the klutzy cat?" So I say "Keep them both, and go home. I pray for my attitude….again.

Sunday morning I look forward to my usual schedule, being at my regular spot at the information booth at church, greeting people at the door. The first one in is

Don Anderson. He asks, "How is the job going"? I say "Oh fine, I was there on Friday." I think the sermon topic was "How to Handle Guilt." After church we go home, eat lunch, and I drag out the theology books, read five minutes, and fall asleep.

I dreamed that I was a full-time, pre-paid Bible college student. My wife was supporting us by taking in washing or something. My days were spent in the library looking up obscure references and astounding the faculty with my great   wisdom.   Everything   being done….decently….and…..in….order….

I finished the one year course "Bible survey" and received my certificate in 1984 at the age of 51. Definitely the oldest freshman in the school.

* * *

4

"Three Generations are all Mother"

By
Katharine Valentino

[**EDITOR'S NOTE**:   *As I near the end of my life, I will tell you my stories.*

What will I tell you? I've lived in Florida, Colorado, Georgia, Texas, Louisiana, California, Indiana, Maryland, Arizona and Oregon—but relocations no longer seem relevant, if they ever were. I've worked as a sales clerk, a waitress, a bartender, a go-go dancer, a writer, an editor, a Website developer and a personal-development life coach—but careers seem inconsequential now. In college, I got almost all A's—but grades seem trivial now. I married (four times, yikes!), but ex-husbands seem ... wait ... two of my husbands were important. They gave me my children.

Ah, yes: As I near the end of my life, I will tell my stories to my children, and to their children, and to theirs.]

* * *

I was born two months premature in 1943 before there was such a thing as neonatal intensive care. In telling the story of my birth, my mother said the medical staff at the hospital acted as though I was expected to die. I was parked in an incubator for a few days, however, and when I didn't die in the hospital I was discharged. Nobody gave my mother instructions as to what special care I might need. She was told only one thing, and that by a nurse: "Doctor says you'll have to bottle feed her."

The long trip home was difficult, Mama said. November, and even in Florida that means 40-degree weather. The car was elderly and unheated. It was raining. There were floods. By the time Daddy got mother and baby into the house, everyone felt cold, damp and exhausted.

Thank goodness for my grandmother and for Nan, my great grandmother.

The house had no central heat, but it did have a fireplace. As Mama tells it, she carried me from a cold car into a living room made warm by a crackling fire. My Gramma and Nan had started the fire, attached a clothesline to the ceiling in a semi-circle in front of it, and hung blankets from the clothesline to the floor. They had brought out my bassinet and put it between the fire and the blankets. Gramma took me from Mama's arms and laid me in that warm space.

I remained next to that fire for weeks. Daddy had to go back to the war, so in addition to all the manual household chores that in the 1940s were necessary to keep a family fed and clean, the three women chopped and brought in wood and kept that fire going. Each woman took an eight-hour shift with me seven days a week, not leaving me alone for even a minute.

Until I got strong enough to suck, Mama told me she used a breast pump to extract her own milk. She fed that milk to me in an eye dropper, drop by drop. To keep me awake long enough even to swallow, Gramma or Nan had to tap the bottoms of my feet while Mama administered the milk.

I stopped breathing three times. The first time, Mama said everyone except Nan panicked. Nan calmly fetched the bottle of whiskey and the eye dropper and placed one drop of that appalling substance on my tongue. The shock brought me back to the living, choking and coughing. Thereafter, the whiskey sat next to my bassinet.

Almost a month from the day I was born, I opened my eyes for the first time and looked at my world. All three women cried.

Mama told me about my birth when I was a teenager, She laughed about how she didn't know what tired was until some time in the third week of that ordeal. When I grew much older, however, I came to fully appreciate the effort these three women, my mother, my grandmother and my great grandmother, made to keep me alive.

* * *

"Equality"

When I was perhaps nine years old, my father was stationed in Lake Charles, Louisiana. Soon after we moved into our house there, other officers' wives suggested to my mother that she hire a Negro maid (when I was a child, "Negro" was the polite term for black people). For some weeks, my mother rejected these suggestions. She could certainly care for her own household and children. She changed her mind, however, when she found out she would only have to pay a dollar an hour for help. A small amount to her, $8 a day would be all a Southern Negro family might have to live on. So, she hired a very nice black lady named Suzy to come clean our house twice a week.

Suzy's first day at our house got interesting. Come lunchtime, for example, Suzy informed us that she had to have a different set of dishes than those we used. My mother had to rummage around to find dishes with a different pattern than ours, so the dishes "fo dah coloreds," as Suzy said, could be kept separate from the dishes "fo dah white people" like us. What she found different was my brother's well-used plastic plate and cup. My brother, who until that day had not known he was white, would not be using his Lone Ranger dishes anymore.

That wasn't all: Suzy also had to have different kitchen and bathroom towels to dry her hands on, which we could no longer use. And, she got to sit in the cheerful kitchen to have lunch, while we had to sit in the dining room, where we had to practice our manners.

My brother and I understood less than nothing about what it meant to be colored, or Negro, in those days. My mother, however, was learning how much damage slavery, poverty and racism had done to this woman who had come into our lives.

Over the next few weeks, my mother tried several times to treat Suzy as an equal, but each time she succeeded only in upsetting her. On these occasions, Suzy would say, "Yes'm, you don unnerstan. Dat be what is." My mother realized she would have to go along with the status quo.

Then came a day my mother would always remember.

It rained that morning, and Suzy showed up with her uniform all wet. My mother asked her how she'd gotten to work and was shocked to learn that the trip from Suzy's home to hers was eight miles, only six of it by bus. For $8, this woman had stood on a crowded bus for six miles and then walked two miles in 90-degree rainy weather. She would then clean house, cook, do laundry and iron all day, and then make the same exhausting trip back home.

At the end of the day, my mother didn't want to hear about any "dis-be-what-is stuff" and insisted upon driving Suzy home. When they arrived at Suzy's little house, they found her son in the front yard. Suzy introduced him: "Miz Senneville maam, dis my son, Larry," she said. "Larry, say hello to Miz Senneville."

Larry stood up very straight and said carefully, "How do you do, Miz Sent-Fill, maam."

My mother replied "Very well, thank you, Larry." And how old are you, may I ask?"

Still ramrod straight, Larry replied "I be ten."

Quick as a flash, Suzy reached out and slapped her son so hard he actually fell in the dust at my mother's feet. "I be ten, MAAM," she commanded. Larry scrambled to his feet, tears in his eyes, and repeated "I be ten, maam."

My mother felt mortified. She turned to Suzy and said, "Surely he doesn't have to say 'maam' to me."

"Yess'm," said Suzy, "but Miz Senneville maam, I know you don unnerstan how it be, but dis here Nigra boy, he learn to say maam to white womens or he wine up in jail or dead. He cannot forgit, ever."

She was absolutely right. Because in the South in 1952, dat be what was. Martin Luther King would not have a dream for another 11 years.

Suzy cleaned our house for five years, until my father got stationed elsewhere. My mother picked her up every morning and took her home every evening that she worked for us. Because in my mother's house, that's the way it was.

5

"Anatomy and Drama of a Biopsy"

By
Julie Woods Olson

[**EDITOR'S NOTE**: *Julie is a fourth generation Oregonian. She grew up in Sherman County on the family wheat farm. She graduated from the University of Oregon in Gerontology and received a Masters in Counseling from Oregon State University. She served in the Peace Corps in Turkey.*]

* * *

November 18, 1991, at age 48, I went for a routine mammogram. The technician looked at my films and asked me to wait for the radiologist. The wait in that cold lonely room seemed interminable.

The thoughts racing through my mind and heart were of my younger sister, Christine, enduring chemotherapy for breast cancer and my second oldest sister, Susan, who at 30 years of age died of an astrocytoma brain tumor.

The radiologist came in and showed me the microcalcifications on the film of my left breast. He referred me to a surgeon, Dr. Sandra Beal.

A week later on November 25, 1991, they performed my biopsy at Sacred Heart Short Stay. My daughter, Megan, 23-years old, a strong woman made of the "stuff" of her mother and grandmother, delivered me to Short Stay, waited and took me home.

In the operating room Dr. Beal agreed to give me my biopsy results that same day if possible. Oh, happy day! The frozen section was benign.

Two days later Dr. Beal checked my incision and drains. All was well. I left her office and drove to my counseling office in Albany.

That same day, at 11 a.m. Dr. Beal received my pathology report. Not able to reach me by phone she called Megan at work telling her that it was malignant. Megan's boss, Michael, found her freaking out and sobbing. She had called my office several times to no avail. Those were the days of land lines. He told her to go to my home and wait for me to arrive.

In shock and devastated over the sudden change in diagnosis, we decided to follow through with our Thanksgiving plans that day with my oldest sister Sherry's family in Eastern Oregon. On the drive along the Columbia River highway I read aloud from Dr. Susan

Love's breast cancer book. Our family was loving and supportive. We were all grieving our other sister's cancers and hoping for the best.

December 2, 1991 I met with my primary physician for a second opinion. She stated that no one treatment was superior over another. She referred me to an oncologist in Eugene who told me my cancer was not serious enough for his attention. Fortunately, an oncologist in Albany agreed to treat me.

The irony of this cancer diagnosis involves the fact that one day previously I had signed up for an AFLAC cancer insurance policy. My agent met me at Dr. Beal's office to get the biopsy report and begin the insurance coverage.

December 3, 1991, my sister Sherry, my daughter, and I met with Dr. Beal to discuss surgical procedures. Christine called from Minnesota wanting to be part of the procedure decision.

My biopsy showed a three mm invasive ductal carcinoma with extensive intraductal component. The intraductal carcinoma extended to the surgical margin of the excision. This type of cancer is positive for estrogen hormone receptor.

December 9, 1991 I had a left modified radical mastectomy. Dr. Beal removed 37 cancer free lymph nodes. My treatment included five years of the cancer drug Tomoxifen. The side effects were menopausal hell.

My sister, Christine, at age 54, died from a recurrence of breast cancer. My daughter, Megan, has breast cancer not only on her maternal side of the family, but her paternal grandmother and great uncle also were diagnosed with breast cancer.

As I write this, the date is May 1, 2013. I am 22 years cancer free. I only think about a possible recurrence when I do my monthly breast exams and my yearly mammogram. I have shared my strength and hope with many women.

My only regret is not having had a double mastectomy.

* * *

Tooth Fairy Magic

On a hot June morning my nine year old grandson and I spent the morning pulling weeds at our church parking lot. Ravenous, we went to Bambinos for a large slice of pizza, salad and a drink. While the owner was waiting on my grandson a lower baby tooth fell out. He saved it while the owner made a big fuss over the loss of his tooth. After eating his pizza he asked for another slice. In a few minutes the owner returned with another slice saying it was from the Tooth Fairy.

6

"The Magic Summers"

By
Paula May

[EDITOR'S NOTE: *Paula May spent 35 years in the field of medicine as a Registered Nurse Administrator. She is now retired. Paula is also a published author of* **"Wisdom from the Heart"** *and presenter of Life Empowerment workshops she has written.*]

* * *

After many, many moves to various houses and new towns throughout my young life we finally settled in a small town named Forest Lake, Minnesota. Our step-father created such a difference in the lives of my mom, brother, sister and my self. We now lived in a real home on a 900 acre farm. With the farm came chores for everyone no matter what the age. My mother chose me to start the household cooking and cleaning at just over nine. This work included cooking all three meals in summer, vacuuming, washing floors, laundry and ironing. I worked very hard every day throughout the year accomplishing these chores with little or no recognition from my mother.

The year I turned ten my new Dad surprised me with a Greyhound bus ticket to visit my mother's parents for two weeks in St. Cloud, Minnesota. He decided I needed a break in my routine, a vacation, which brought me tears of happiness. No one had ever done such a nice thing for me before, especially trusting me to travel alone.

The excitement built up day by day as the week of preparation flew by, carrying me along with that energy. I eagerly ran around collecting clothing to place in the well worn Samsonite case belonging to my mother. The composition of that case was a version of hard plastic, making it so very heavy, I couldn't carry it downstairs from my second floor bedroom, and had to ask my dad for help.

Just when the anticipation had built to a crescendo, making me breathless, the day finally arrived for departure. Dad drove me into town to wait at the bus stop since we had no actual depot. As the bus pulled in, it was the biggest vehicle I had ever seen and the loudest, but I looked forward to my new adventure with deep happiness. I gave my ticket to the driver who told me to sit in the first front facing seat behind him so he could keep track of me in his rearview mirror. I promptly sat next to the open window. As we rolled away the breeze began blowing my long hair around my face. No air conditioning existed on buses in those days, so the outside breeze helped keep the air inside balanced.

My German grandparents, Sophia and Joseph Rau, were meeting me at the Greyhound station in St. Cloud early that Saturday evening. Uncle Alex, my mother's brother, drove us all home in his car so we didn't have to walk. Once he dropped us off, grandma said it was time to relax before supper would be served. Wow, I never had time to relax before supper before. What a nice change. All of a sudden it dawned on me for the next two weeks I could just be a ten year old girl receiving lots of attention from loving grandparents.

The next day, a Sunday, we dressed in our best clothes, Grandma in her hat with the small blue feather, Grandpa in his suit and tie, me in my brilliant lilac and purple, ruffled dress. Of course we walked uptown to St. Mary's Cathedral since my grandparents never owned a car. During that leisurely stroll we said "hi" to everyone we met because they all knew Sophie and Joe Rau. Sun shone down in a warm light as a gentle slight breeze passed around us all as we slowly wended our way into town.

The outside of the cathedral shone with a very imposing, glittery façade built of Minnesota granite sparkling in the mid-morning sun. Inside, barely containing my excitement, I gawked like a first time tourist. Heavenly sounds from the choir drifted throughout the huge, heavily adorned interior. My grandparents struggled to remind me to be very quiet. It wasn't because I forgot my manners, but, I never before attended mass without having to take care of my two younger siblings, thus bypassing all the beauty that surrounded the parishioners.

After mass as we started down the broad steps, the giant Carllion bells, began their sweet call to the next mass and the Monsignor made sure to say hello to me. Walking happily between Sophie and Joe, they suddenly veered towards the long block of shops, which included a German Bakery emitting delightful aromas of fresh baked goods. Ordering both a fresh white loaf and a fresh rye loaf of bread I thought we were done, but grandma said I could order a large sugar cookie iced in half chocolate and half vanilla for after dinner, plus to my delight the owner put in two more for the next day.

On our way home, Sophie and Joe said they had a surprise that would make me very happy. Just then Grandpa said, "Polly take those steps down below the sidewalk."

Doing so, I went through the door. I noticed at the bottom a fancy gold painted sign saying, "Ebreckens German pub. Upon entering my legs automatically stopped moving of their own accord as I tried to take in everything my senses could handle all at one time. The huge room completely festooned with bright light in antique fixtures that were turn of the century, overlaid with stained glass shone from every wall.

Along the right wall ran a full length dark polished Oak bar with sturdy red leather covered stools. Filled with men and women dressed in their Sunday finest clothes, everyone laughed and talked in a mixture of German and English. The smell of cigarettes and flavorful pipe tobaccos wafted to the door area. In the center of the room were tables of all sizes encircled by chairs, while along the left wall comfortable booths lined up invitingly. We sat in a booth. The many waitresses of all ages, came quickly to help us, each of them extremely happy. The reason for this stop made itself clear as my gaze finally wandered to the back of the room fitted with two stoves and two refrigerators. From the stoves emanated mouth watering aromas of the best smelling beef roast and gravy.

We were here for dinner, consisting of hot roast beef sandwiches on homemade bread, including mashed potatoes, both covered in dark, rich beef gravy. The sides consisted of generous additions of fresh corn on the cob and home made coleslaw. I couldn't believe my good fortune to only eat and not cook this fantastic meal. My icy cold drink of choice, Grape Crush, tasted tangy and fresh on my tongue. Grandpa drank a Boch beer and Grandma drank beer with 7-up added which she called a 'Cincinnati." In those days there were no rules for banning children from a bar/restaurant. This family-owned pub, carried a genuine family atmosphere supported by its clean, sawdust covered floor. This became the best dinner of my youthful memories.

We strolled back to their home. The lower half of a huge house, while only a one bedroom home, they cleverly created a big bedroom with all the amenities from what had been the formal dining room. Old linoleum covered all the floors with grandma's handmade rag rugs laid around the furniture to chase away the chill of Minnesota winters. Outside grandpa's love of gardening showed with the multi-colored primroses growing around the perimeter and the small verdant, abundant vegetable garden bursting with color.

An old dirt floored backyard shed contained several tall crockery jars, heaped to the brim with homemade dill pickles, sour kraut, head cheese, (Pork packed in aspic) pickled pigs feet, homemade root beer and the heavy, aromatic aroma of fresh Dill. Heavy wooden lids weighed down each jar as the processes worked their magic, bringing to fruition delicious food for the winter season.

My grandparents married when Sophie turned 16 and Joe 20 years old. Her father only allowed her to finish the eighth grade in school. All of the grandchildren learned very quickly to pay close attention when playing cards with her because her affinity for numbers was legend in the family. When playing cards she counted our cards and hers faster than anyone in the game. She worked for my uncle as a manager/bookkeeper in his flooring store for many years. Grandpa worked for the Great Northern Railway making box cars for 20 years and before that worked ten years in the granite pits. They loved each other very much and each did delegated chores and duties in the house with Sundays being the day to cook dinner. He took the bus to and from the rail yard everyday. When I stayed there I would walk up to the bus stop to meet him and carry his big old black, round topped, metal lunch box home for him.

Food in the Rau household consisted basically of German dishes, such as coleslaw, hot potato salad, wilted lettuce with hot bacon dressing, pork and beef roasts, and pork chops with homemade applesauce dressing. Needless to say none of this came from a deli market.

Summer nights we all played cards (including we kids) for hours on end on the very large, very well used round, oak kitchen table. I realize now we all got so many things from that home--entertainment, a sense of family, friends, lessons in math, respect and a feeling of belonging to something far greater then ourselves.

Every day of those two weeks felt magical to me and reminded me that childhood could really be fun. Leaving my grandparents always tugged at my heart, just as I knew they would miss my presence as well. For three summers I completely enjoyed my sojourns to St. Cloud with Grandma Sophie, and Grandpa Joe. I would also miss sleeping with the mournful sound of train whistles sounding their songs to faraway destinations to someone else's magical moments, and I missed saying my prayers every night in German.

7

"The Life That Awaits Me"

By
Thomas Oroyan

[**EDITOR'S NOTE:** *Retired architect Thomas Oroyan, was born in Hawaii, attended the University of Hawaii and the University of Oregon. He has lived in Oregon for over 40 years. His wife, gael, instigated and facilitated this class of writers' memoir book. Fellow writers fondly tease Thomas as the "teacher's pet!"*]

* * *

Under balmy and sunny skies one late August Sunday, during the summer of 1998, while attending a Family Reunion in Hawaii, I found out that I had inherited Muscular Dystrophy. An older brother, retired from the army had just had a physical at the local military hospital there. He said I needed to see his doctor to verify and compare conditions regarding a nerve/muscular disease. It turns out to be a disease that males of the family inherited from my mother, bless her soul...I pray she did not take it too hard when she received the news in heaven. I did pray to her for support to give me the strength to endure this disease for I never felt so scared in my life; for the life that awaits me.

The news was hard to take although at the time, I could think of only a few symptoms related like: nervousness, tremors, hoarseness, and poor muscle development. My particular MD condition is diagnosed as an adult type onset disease. At the moment, there is no cure. At age 60 then, I thanked God and felt fortunate that I was able to have at least enjoyed my childhood and young adult life with its related ambulatory activities. When Susie, my late wife at the time, and I researched the disease and poured over info found on the internet and in books, my anxiety heightened. Although with care and therapy, many with this disease can live "normal lives" into a ripe old age; many will see the early symptoms mentioned worsen. Falling and balance problems often ensure that future regular use of a wheelchair is most likely inevitable.

I felt concerned for our future and pondered ways to minimize hardship, financially, mentally and physically. I worried especially about Susie, how she'd manage and what our growing older together and retirement would be like. I tried getting Long Term Care Insurance but was denied because of the pre-existing disease. Strange that the same insurance company accepted my wife and her dad with pre-existing coronary conditions. My guess is that I may live too long costing more to an insurance company. Annual physical exams noted good health until recently.

Then, the impact in my worry in how to handle my own disease while dealing with another emergency reached its crescendo. In January of 2000, Susie received a diagnosis of colon cancer, devastating news. Susie, at the height of her career was enjoying life, as an internationally known Doll Artist and Author. She created one of a kind Art Dolls, had one-woman shows. Her dolls were featured in museums including the Louvre. She wrote best selling doll books, taught classes and traveled. It was hard on Susie but she kept an upper lip as best she could. On good days, she worked, wrote and attended related events up to six months before her passing. She suffered for seven years but hardly complained.

Juggling between work and caring for Susie became hectic. I was into my fourth year of employment as Campus Architect with Lane Community College when her illness began. Bless Lane and computer technology for allowing me to work at home to be with Susie and still keep up campus related matters. Bless mother-in-law Eunice and Care Giver Lacey for attending to Susie especially during some weekday mornings when I had to be away to attend meetings. Although caring for Susie was challenging, I would do it again because of my love for her.

I had a lot of good help. Most times I managed to tackle a lot of the home chores and caring for Susie. I learned to be a better cook to accommodate Susie's appetite and mine. She would yell out cooking instructions from the bedroom. It was a real experience when I did my first turkey. I mastered which buttons to push or pull when doing laundry, and I ironed clothes and cleaned the house the best I could. After lessons from visiting nurses I could bathe Susie in her bed when needed and do the necessary change and cleaning of her colostomy conditions.

The vows I took when we married, "in sickness and in health" rang constantly through my head. My belief is that's what a marriage is all about and what a husband would do without question. Matters gradually became a hardship as I felt my own disease exacerbating from normal body efforts tending to Susie and my own needs. My body took a toll. I felt my strength reaching peak. But you know, I felt proud and it felt good that I could be her champion when demanding, fighting for better services that she deserved and should have from doctors, nurses, etc. It felt good that I managed to keep her at home, as she requested, during her remaining days on earth. On her last day, she received the Holy Sacrament, and on her last night, she died in my arms, in our bed, and in the house she loved.

I felt certain that all the hardships became challenges, giving me the courage and strength, in time, to move forward through grief and grieving toward a new life. In spring of 2010, my new life began. I reconnected with gael, a high school classmate, and now my present wife. I was hesitant about how she would respond at our first meeting, seeing a much older classmate with a cane. She didn't flinch, as she'd been made aware of my MD from the very beginning of our "love e-mail exchanges." We reached for each other's hands at our first dining date and at the end, she was the first woman to lead me out of a restaurant after placing my hand on her shoulder for support. A year later we married.

After nearly two years of marriage and a year and half into retirement, my MD has progressed to a point that I myself must admit that I will be dependent on help, on gael, even more. I feel the use of a wheelchair becoming closer as a needed apparatus. I hate it but my body and my legs say otherwise. Lately, at times, I have become somewhat bitter, angry, and jealous of those who still enjoy walking and dancing. "Why me?" I ask...."Could be worse." The answer subconsciously sometimes hits me in the face. Just be thankful.....believe me I am. Especially when I am with my loving wife gael, I am trying and learning to be patient, to accept the circumstances and live with it.

I find my MD has not stopped us from enjoying and planning a happy, memorable life. For the past two years we have been trying to make the most of our brand new life together. We have been involved with traveling, enjoying performing arts and other community activities. We've kept busy and active. However, we also treasure much the solitude together, games, reading, movies and TV watching or just relishing quiet lunches. We love reminiscing while visiting along the beaches of Hawaii and the coast of Oregon that brings forth nostalgia of our youth and growing up in the islands.

I know that in the years to come, we will have new challenges to deal with for sure. gael has been heaven sent. She has excelled in meeting her own personal challenges besides coping with me, my idiosyncrasies and progressing disease in our fairy tale life together. I pray I am able to be worthy of this wonderful woman for it's a challenge to live with a man whose life has changed in so many ways since that fateful day announcing the dreadful news of muscular dystrophy, changing my life forever.

* * * *

Competing With Bygones, Exes and Beaus

When gael said she would marry me I thought I finally hit the mother lode of unrequited love and happiness. Nothing can go wrong, I thought. Trivia matters will be brushed easily aside. However, I forgot for a while that sometimes, some people like me dizzy with "new love" initially become possessive and react with envy against any competition be it past, present or future.

Six months into our engagement, I gradually learned more about gael. We shared our past histories and commonalities. gael brought me a bunch of photos as I had asked. I wanted to start an album showing a gradation of past life photos of gael as a child, as I knew her in high school, as she grew to maturity with family and careers and as I know her today. She even brought me her personal journals written over the years. She was and still is, so open, so trusting with nothing to hide, loving life and people.

The photos of gael were great except for one. She had included a large photo of her and ex-beau Fred— from our high school days. It was a colored photo posed chest up, showing matching aloha attire, made by gael's mom. Though I knew the photo was of by gone days, I could not help being jealous and mad. Heck, I was still fresh from reading some of gael's early journals when she was in high school and going steady with Fred. At times, her teenage writing was mushy and pukish with all that baby or Elmer Fudd like-talk, how she adored "Fweddy's so cute and always weddy" with his coordinated outfit of the day. I guess she was in love then, too, I thought, still mad with jealousy. Mind you, she went steady with him for four years (never did anything serious. "I was a good Catholic girl," she said).

In contrast, I was a good Catholic boy but I did everything I thought or wanted to.

To ease the pain, and with great glee, I took a black magic marker and drew and noted all over Fred's side of the photo. I then put the marked photo back into the 10 x 11 cardboard folder with the flipped back cover and forgot about it until I returned some photos back to gael. As gael kind of perused through what she got back, she noticed the large photo cardboard frame closed so she opened it. I did not see her facial reaction as I was in the next room when I heard this shrieking squeal. Just then, realizing it was her reaction to the marked photo, I hurried to her. I quickly told her to calm down and pulled out the untouched original photo hidden behind the marked photo copy. Instantly we both burst out laughing in relief. I told her it ticked me to read about Fred in her journal and again when I saw the nifty photo of them I went ballistic. She understood, felt flattered and told me not to worry about her bygone days with former beaus and that her Irish eyes are for me only. However, she did explain her reaction to such a jealous deed. When she saw the unflattering markings on the photo, she lost her breath in horror, "Can it be that her new love, me, would have the gall to graffiti her personal memorable photo?" She continued to share her thoughts of me at the moment which went something like "the nerve of that jealous idiot" or something similar.

gael, in fun, I think, mentioned she would show ex-beau Fred the marked up photo copy and tell the story at the upcoming class reunion. She never did. In fact at the reunion with its week of activities we mingled with classmates and ran into Fred and wife Gale (spelled different from my wife gael) several times. In fact we sat together at the picnic, socialized at the sock hop dance, luau party and other functions. We talked at length about the Native American artwork Fred does and his wife's quilting. We talked about architecture and my career in the field and gael's work as Hawaii's Department of Education state director of communication and her post retirement career in writing and teaching.

You know what? When finally confronting the ex-beau, I didn't feel threatened at all nor did any jealousy come forth. In fact, our meeting was somewhat pleasant. I found Fred very easy talk with and his wife delightful. His wife was in awe and complimentary of gael's hula dancing and outfit the night of the Luau. gael looked stunning in her aquamarine colored full length sari-like muumuu that contrasted nicely against her fair skin. She and the dress flowed as one as she danced to the music, Kauai. Mesmerized classmates sang along in unison the popular and lovely hula song. gael's hula ended with great applause and across the way I could see Fred and wife applauding vigorously. After her dance, gael came straight to me. I congratulated her as she kissed me lightly on the lips. I felt proud indeed. Yes, as I told a nearby classmate that night, "It was me who finally married the student body president."

I felt I had confronted the problem by meeting the enemy head on. I have seen the whites of his eyes and found he is no real threat. He appears less foreboding, not as tall as the 6' 4" I remembered, less hair than me and he sported a six-month pregnant belly look. Like all the males at the class reunion and like me, we have aged. To be kind and truthful, I found Fred to be still cordial and the gentleman he was when I knew him in high school and probably why gael felt so attracted to him. We ended our meeting with the traditional Hawaiian style of hugs and kisses, when Fred's wife turned to gael saying "It's ok to give him a big hug," I didn't even flinch.

After almost a year of engagement and nearly two years of marriage, will I still find it challenging to compete with gael's other bygones, former exes and beaus? "I'll try my darndest!!!"

* * *

First Cruise, a Memorable One

My travel to Alaska by ship occurred in the fall of 2010 and I consider it special. The cruise not only marked a first for me but also celebrated a commitment event.

I had done some traveling with my late wife but we never cruised. We thought about it, dreamed about it, but never got the chance. Family members who've experienced cruises to Europe and elsewhere raved and encouraged us that a cruise was the best way to travel and to at least try it once in your life time. So I felt excited when the opportunity came along..... I met gael.

When gael and I decided to get serious as a loving couple, we thought it neat to announce our commitment, engagement on a cruise. gael had been on numerous cruises and talked about her wonderful experiences. She thought that the Alaskan cruise would be the best intro for me. She was right. Her sister Jana, an ordained minister joined us and administered the vows of commitment during the voyage. I thought it so unusual, so romantic.

However, I felt in awe of the whole trip. It smacked of luxury. I felt it was not me. I don't belong here I thought to myself....too rich for my blood......But boy, once I got the taste of it, I liked it. If this offered a sense of how the rich and famous lived.....I could live like this. There appears to be a balance of excitement and relaxation that's appealing. If only I was wealthy enough to continue experiencing this cruise life. gael said she's done it and is not rich. She hopes to continue her cruising adventures with me. That is, as long as God allows us to be healthy enough to travel. She noted that's what retirement or the golden years are all about. That if one saved properly and planned wisely, an annual wonderful life of cruise traveling is possible and can be realized.

From the port of Seattle the cruise pattern paralleled the scenic edge of Alaska, stopping along picturesque cities and towns. The cruise climaxed at a turning point that featured the magnificent Mendenhall Glacier near the city of Juneau where we even spotted a couple of whales. Also in Juneau, we visited the famous Red Dog Saloon, a place hard to forget with antiques, posters, saw dust floor and a lively piano player. And yes, their featured Duck Fart beer....no, we never tried it. We stuck to typical ordinary draft beer. gael and sister Jana enjoyed the walk to the edge of town where totem poles stood as a major attraction. In the city of Ketchikan, we were amused by the preserved old section of town that featured boardwalks to various shops and the famous Dolly's House of ill repute frequented by many lonely men in the old days, now a museum of interest and enjoyed by many tourists.

During the week and half cruise on the Holland America ship, by its mere hugeness, it felt like being in a compact resort city. Like high rises with multi-layers, comprised of stream-lined promenade decks, swanky cabin quarters, various event rooms and complimented by the interior shops, a casino, spas and neat private areas, not to mention the informal eating areas and elegant dining rooms with live music boasting a king's menu in many ways. The libations and variety of great food proved just outstanding. The steaks were great; however I think I exceeded my limits in healthy omega 3 by over indulging in delicious lox and lobster dishes almost daily.

Some Miscellaneous side adventures and discoveries:

We enjoyed the night club-like shows that easily matched Las Vegas in levels of performances.

Though green with envy, but knowing gael loves to dance, I allowed a guy to dance with her at the sock hop night..and damn, if that same guy didn't ask her to dance the next night at a piano bar session. The several piano bars entertained with excellent music throughout the ship. One even played some Hawaiian music. gael danced the hula to a couple of songs and received loud applause.

The long walks to various destinations were tough on me and my legs...however, we finally got smart and rented a wheelchair and with gael's toughness (she pushed), life improved...I/we learned....and next time I/we vowed to rent a scooter.

My balance problem:

Coming out of the port in Seattle, the sea rocked roughly and the ship seemed to rock fairly hard.....I lost my balance and fell backwards hitting the deck solid on my butt followed by my poor head. gael's sister Jana, a retired nurse, told me to stay put until the ship medics arrived. They took me by wheelchair to the ship doctor's office. After the Doc examined me, being concerned about concussion, gael asked what she needed to be aware of. The Doc, with prior knowledge of our fairy tale love story and engagement, did not skip a beat.......He turned to gael and said..."If he starts kissing the lamp post instead of you, bring him back to my office."

I learned another thing. Over the counter sea sick pills work. Ship's doc gave me some complimentary packages that if bought would be ten times less expensive than prescription.

"Will I cruise again?....Yes sir!"

Summer of 2011 we took a week long cruise around the Hawaiian Islands.

Future cruise planned: Early Summer 2013, 14 day cruise / 3 days at South Hampton/London to visit with family then on to a two- week cruise to ports in Portugal and Spain.

Further future cruises....you betcha!

8

"Dandy Boots"

By
Jim Newell

[EDITOR'S NOTE: *Jim is an ancient retired music store owner who now designs and builds an occasional contra base horn—just to stay off the streets!*]

* * *

The Sears Roebuck listing says "Boys' 10-inch boots." They came with a pocket knife and a knife pocket. The fine print said so: "knife with 1 ¾ and 2-inch blades, celluloid handle engraved with your name, and snap flap pocket."

First class! It didn't matter to me if the boots had soles or heels; they had a knife.

Money was scarce as hens' teeth, but both my brother and I did need boots. Mom had even said *"Both boys will need boots if this winter is like the last."* So she was easy to talk into the very boots we wanted. Patterns were made, mom drawing carefully around our feet, and a letter with a 3-cent stamp affixed was sent off with a money order enclosed.

It only took several days for the boots to arrive, but it seemed an eternity. They were dandy boots. My brother and I were thrilled. By hiking up my trouser leg a bit, I could access the flap with the snap and have my two-bladed knife out and open in the shake of a lamb's tail.

Friends were impressed, and I found no end of knife projects to whittle. I made 15 or 20 barnyard animals, which I glued onto bases. "Old MacDonald" and me.

Even holding my knife in my hand was a satisfying feeling—until the day I reached for the flap and the knife was gone. Oh dear! Self recrimination, guilt, sorrow!

Weeks later, the knife turned up in a dark corner of the house. From then on, I was very careful with it. You know, I still have it in the top drawer of my dresser.

* * *

"My Best and Worst Thanksgiving All Rolled into One"

In the middle of the Great Depression, my parents had eight mouths to feed and not much money. However, the family boasted two mighty-hunter sons, and those sons—Bob and Jack—had recently shot eight Hungarian partridges.   On our old wood-burning kitchen range, Mother prepared traditional festive veggies, sweet spuds, mashed potatoes with gravy, homemade cranberry jelly, relishes and a huge platter of golden brown partridges with golden paper fringed cuffs all poking up in the air. And if that weren't enough chopping and peeling and mashing and stirring and stoking of fire, Mother also made, from scratch, venison minced meat and pumpkin pies.

Being a young boy with friends talking of turkey, I realized that our meal was the only one in town with what I thought of as ordinary partridge shot out in the sagebrush and scabrock. I felt deprived.

It only took a few short years of maturing for me to realize what a gourmet feast Mother had prepared and served in our humble home.

9

"A New Chapter"

By
gael Doyle-Oroyan

[**EDITOR'S NOTE:** *gael retired from the State of Hawaii as Communications Director for the Department of Education in 1994. She's published several children's books (**Surfer Boy, Hula Girl,** and **Haole Girl**), and a novel (**Cinderella's Croning**) under her previous name gael Mustapha. She's also written personality and travel features as well as grand-parenting, humor, and recipe columns for newspapers in addition to teaching a variety of writing classes in colleges and senior centers.*]

* * *

You finish your memoirs, and guess what? Life goes on; often in ways you never dreamed possible.

The challenges, ups, downs, and all arounds keep happening. That's certainly the case in my life; definitely requiring a "new chapter."

I finished Tutu's Tales in September of 2006, (*tutu* is the Hawaiian word for grandmother) ending with the move into the little old school house apartment in Charleston, OR. Since then, life has taken many totally unexpected turns.

This included a blindsiding divorce, a subsequent gypsy lifestyle saga, and a reconnection with a high school classmate, ultimately moving forward into a new marriage with the wedding in Hawaii (my third marriage there). I truly believe the third time's the charm.

And there's much, much, more. Consequently, there is a need to write this new chapter. Let's begin with the divorce.

End of That Road

To keep this part short, (I now call him "X," left me.) I'd gone to Tacoma to see Caitlin give birth to my great-granddaughter Jillian in July '08. She's a little doll.

I flew home to Coos Bay. X picked me up at the airport, took me to the Plank House, one of our favorite restaurants overlooking the Bay for dinner. There he dropped the bomb; told me he was leaving me for a younger woman he'd met on line.

Shock! Anger! Disbelief! No need for lots of details. He'd planned to just leave a note on the kitchen table and go but Meg, a mutual friend, convinced him he couldn't do that.

We got the fastest divorce on record—three days; no custody, property disputes or kids to fight over. I put him on a bus to TN…told him to let me know when he died so I can collect his social security since we'd been married more than ten years (28 years to be exact). I also told him I hoped he'd learn to communicate.

I wrote this poem that sums it up:

"It Hurts"

You walked on my heart,
Leaving dirty footprints
After a very great, long-ago start.
It causes me to ache, wince.

So many super good years,
Laughter, joy, grand world travel.
Happiness, good memories, few tears…
How did it all so fast unravel?

You never gave hints, Dude
That things for you weren't right.
Communication lack, no change in mood,
Nothing visible or obvious in sight.

The woman in that chat room,
Totally unbelievable to me.
Maybe a leech witch on a broom
Time will tell, you'll see.

I'd like to kick you in the head.
Anger and emotions broil
Make me mad. I won't wish you dead,
To a higher plane I'm loyal.
So much to deal with, so hard…

Moving, money, madness, mayhem and mess.
Many think of you now as a real retard,
A scumbag, a loser, and even less.

I've got to get it out, spit, be done,
Cry, wash away all the pain.
It's time for me to move on.
There's yet so much in this world to gain.

I will truly try to accept feeling
Up and down. I must forgive, let go
As I embrace a new chapter, healing.
Only I can and will make it so.

It hurts but I will, seek, find rebirth
Through family, music, friends, harmony
On this very special earth.
I can and will make it happen for me.

Gypsy Life

I lived a gypsy lifestyle as I worked through the grief
process   resulting   from   the   totally   unexpected

abandonment. I went through anger, frustration, confusion, hurt and more. I lived with my daughter, Cathi and her husband, Roy for a time, then at my son, Keith and Teri Ann's. The kids lovingly and wisely said, "Take a year or so Mom, to figure out what you want to do next." I appreciated their support. Keith and Cathi came to Coos Bay to help me move, putting stuff in storage after garage sales. I threw away at least two tubs of my writing clips; cried about that. Stored stuff at grandson Andy's.

Then, I stayed with my sister Jana, her husband Bill, and our Mother for a time. There were good times. Before Bill passed, he, Jana, and I went to England, Ireland (at last), Scotland, Wales, and France. Hope to go back again to the land of my roots in the future.

I felt very loved but also felt I was a burden. I played Bingo frequently in Dublin, CA. A fellow player asked me to join him for lunch; a first date since the divorce. It felt strange, silly...I hadn't "dated" anyone for nearly three decades. We went out several times. He was a gentleman; kissed me once and held me tight in his arms, asked if I thought we might get serious. I wanted to know what "serious" meant to him. He replied, "Long term...maybe some sex..." That scared me. I wasn't ready. Ultimately, before going back to Tacoma, I knew he was a nice guy but not for me.

Gypsy life continued. I thoroughly enjoyed traveling to Arizona and then on to Alaska with Barb and Dorothy.

Read Vikki Stark's *Runaway Husbands* book. Amazing to learn how many men do just what X did. So sad. I think part of it is the "I married you for life, not for lunch" idea. When you're together so much in retirement, it can be hard.

Went back to Jana's when I learned of Bill's illness to help with him and Mother. So sad. Bill and Jana loved each other so much. The lung cancer did him in. He passed peacefully at home with Hospice. Beautiful memorial service. Fortunately, he wasn't sick for long.

Lived through his kids' disgusting greed and rude behaviors. Called police on them. Had never done anything like that before. Glad Jana decided to sell the house and move closer to her kids in northern CA. She found a lovely home in Windsor, a little Victorian village, pop. 25,000 in wine country. New home and no further contact with Bill's kids other than through her lawyer.

We decided I'd live with Jana and Mother and own a tiny percent of the house. My name got put on the deed. I'd join them after my trip back from Tacoma where I'd committed to teach two creative writing classes.

Easter Card Starts New Day

While back at Cathi's, I sent out a funny Easter card e-mail about "what I'd learned from the Easter Bunny" to a number of people including Thomas, a former Kailua High School classmate. He'd lost his wife, Susie, about three years ago (colorectal cancer). I'm not even sure why I sent it to him, but had thought about him, wondered how he was doing. We'd e-mailed a time or two before. He hadn't attended the 50th reunion because Susie had just passed away.

I was curious to find out if he'd remarried…some other classmates did. I also figured the Easter Bunny might provide a little joy for him. He'd once before asked about all of us getting together when passing through Eugene to see my cousin, Rita. We never did that.

Thomas responded to the Easter Bunny e-mail, glad to be back in touch. That started a month-long e-mail marathon. I learned Thomas had a crush on me in high school but was too shy to ever let me know "because of that big guy always by your side." We'd worked together on the yearbook and the Kai High Surfrider newspaper. He did the logo and art work used in both publications which I edited.

As Thomas said about our e-mails, an archaeologist would wonder what language we communicated in--- English, Gaelic, Tagalog, Visayan and lots of Pidgin. What fun! We shared so much. He sent flowers, not once but twice. This all led to the potential of a real in person reconnection in Eugene this time. It happened sooner rather than later as the classes I was to teach got cancelled because not enough students signed up. At least I was able to stay through Cathi's hysterectomy. She recovered well and fast in spite of a problem and having to come home with a catheter that had to stay in for about two weeks.

On the way to Eugene, I stayed one night with old friend and former student, Madge. Had lunch with Aunt Lura and Uncle LaVerne the next day and then drove through Salem, lots of rain and on to Eugene. Stayed with cousin Rita one night. Larry was away re-roofing their cabin. We agreed to go out to dinner; asked Thomas to join us at P.F. Chang's. Rita served as chaperone.

Thomas had told me, "Hawaiian style, you know--you owe me kisses for the flowers." When we finally met at the restaurant, I handed him a small plastic bag of chocolate candy kisses. He pocketed them quickly and pulled me into his arms. We kissed, a first. It felt so warm, embracing, friendly and loving. He later told me he wanted to pull me away from Rita and take me home that first night.

The next morning I headed to his house for a three-night stay. Like wow *laulau*. It was totally unbelievable, unexpected fairytale magic!! I'd never dreamed of being with a man again, let alone, falling madly, crazily in love. The big *kahuna* must have been directing this. It happened fast, in about six weeks, from first reconnect to major skin on skin loving commitment and yes, to engagement. Wowie! Is this for real?

Although I never expected to get involved with a man again, I've always been a believer in the philosophy that when one door closes another opens. That seems to be exactly what was happening.

I will continue to record our future as it happens. As they say, life isn't over until the fat lady sings at your memorial service. And, I feel we are far from over at this point.

The "commitment/engagement" ring we selected together arrived with more flowers and our telephone calls continued. The ring (diamonds and emeralds) is beautiful. Our e-mails and phone calls continued as we fell more and more deeply in love.

I wrote a *"Fairy Tales for All Ages"* piece about our story that was published in the August-September (2010) issue of **Book Women**. I went up to visit again over the July 4 weekend; there five days. Thomas had made a "loving" schedule and planned events—meeting Eunice, dinner with her, a Cabaret Theatre program, luncheons, and more around his spread sheet literally. Haha. What fun. I know—too much info (TMI).

Living in separate places, commuting and meeting up like on our great cruise to Alaska where Jana seriously thought about having us committed rather than doing our "commitment ceremony" were challenges but we knew like the Il Divo song, "someday, somewhere, there's a place for us."

That was just the beginning. We found it, were married in Hawaii in a fantastic gathering with friends, relatives, and classmates. Jana did the ceremony.

Now we've been married over two years. There is much more to come.

10

"Two Black Cats and the Red Velvet Settee"

By
Eunice Scruggs

[**EDITOR"S NOTE**: *Eunice Scruggs is a cat lady a quilter, and a retired housewife, if a housewife ever retires. At one time, she taught ballet. She lives in Eugene, OR and finds her ninth decade as busy and stimulating as all those decades before.*]

* * *

It was a cold, stormy November day. The wind tossed the bare oak tree limbs into all sorts of tormented shapes and blew gusts of rain sideways against the sliding glass doors.

Inside, all was cozy and warm. I happily moved about the kitchen doing some pre-Christmas baking. Soft music from my favorite classical music station played on the radio. In the living room on the red velvet settee, Mildred, also known as Girl Cat, lay curled up in a black fur circle, sleeping the sleep of the just.

I happened to look out the window and there on the deck, hunkered down in a tight-knit package, a cat huddled against the storm. Sydney, A.K.A Boy Cat, Mildred's brother, lay there.

I hurried to the door to let him in. He greeted me with his usual polite "meow." I never knew if he was saying "hello" or "thank you" when he did that. I did appreciate his courtesy.

After patiently submitting to having his muddy paws wiped, Boy Cat went immediately into the kitchen to check up on his food dish of course, to make sure some food remained. That done, he strolled into the living room and sat down in the center of the rug and gave himself a thorough, all-over wash.

Then, it came time to decide just where he would settle in for his six-hour midday nap. After eyeing every piece of furniture in the room, he apparently decided that Girl Cat had made the right decision—the red velvet settee had to be the place. He obviously had no intention of sharing it with her.

He walked over to the red velvet settee, jumped up, and batted his sister off onto the floor. She, hardly awake when she landed, looked up at him, seeming a bit dazed. Boy Cat glared back at her in that silent concentrated stare with which cats seem to decide issues. His look plainly reminded Girl Cat that he, the Alpha Male in this household, had first preference to whatever he wanted.

And since he wanted the red velvet settee, he had every right to it. Then, he gave his chest two licks with his bright pink tongue, curled up into a flat black fur circle, wrapped his beautiful fluffy tail around himself, gave a deep sigh and went to sleep.

Girl Cat sat in the middle of the living room carpet, her back to the red velvet settee. Her rigid back, laid back ears and whiskers sticking straight out from each side of her beautiful face expressed her fury. Her fluffy black tail, even more beautiful than her brother's, swished angrily from side to side.

She stood up, turned, and glared at sleeping Boy Cat. Then, she stalked across the rug, jumped up onto the red velvet settee, and gave him two fierce slaps with her paw.

"Right on, sister!" I yelled out, delighted to see this demonstration of feline women's lib. Boy Cat woke, startled to see his sister standing over him with paw upraised, claws extended, ready to strike again if necessary.

It turned out not to be necessary. Boy Cat evidently knew he'd done wrong, that this time, he'd gone too far. He meekly lowered himself from the red velvet settee and slunk off down the hall to the den, his tail at half-mast.

Girl Cat watched him. Then she gave her chest two licks with her bright pink tongue, curled herself up into a flat black fur circle on the red velvet settee, wrapped her beautiful   fluffy black tail, more beautiful than her brother's, around herself. She gave a deep sigh and went to sleep.

My pride in her actions swelled. That's my recollection of my two black cats and the red velvet settee.

* * *

"The Ballet Studio"

The William F. Christenson School of Ballet, Portland, Oregon, 1935. It's a warm summer evening. The studio is a long dim room; the only light coming from the floor to ceiling French windows at the far end. The windows face north on Tenth Street. The setting sun's long rays and yellow light slant down the canyon of the street and reflect off the buildings across the way. The long sheer curtains wave gently in the warm breeze drifting through the tall open windows.

At the piano, Lucy Giovanetti, our accompanist, intently watches the maestro, Mr. Christenson, as he paces back and forth, eyes on the floor, hand sketching the movements of the choreography of the next combination he wants us to do. We are so fortunate to have an artist of Lucy's quality at the piano. Although not a dancer herself, she has the gift to find instantly the music with not only the right two/four, waltz, four/four or six/eight beat, but also the right phasing and always, music by the world's finest composers.   For the rest of our lives, whether we are listening at home or in the car to the local classic music station, or even all dressed up, attending a formal symphony concert, when we hear those strains that Lucy played, we may seem to be sitting quietly but inside our skin, we are dancing, dancing.

We dancers are standing, slouched, still breathing hard from the last combination. We are each wrapped in that warm, sweaty looseness that tells us our bodies are ready to try anything.

"Okay," says Mr. C., "From the corner…" and he outlines a combination full of the great leaps (grand jetes, sautés de basque) and jumping turns (tours jetes, tours en l'air) that are so much fun. To the Chopin waltz, one by one, we fly across that huge room from one end to the other in just four measures.

Mr. C. will murmur a soft, "Don't let that back foot droop," or "a deeper plié will give you a higher jump." He never raises his voice at his dancers, and when he says the one word, "Good!" with a half-smile, it is as good as getting an Oscar.

Whenever I hear a Chopin or Schubert waltz, especially if it has been recorded in a room with an echo, I am instantly 15 again, back in that warm, dim studio, waiting my turn to dance.

* * *

"The Day That Changed My Life"

"When you love someone, he is your life. The first principle of existence, and because of that he has the power to change you and everything you know."

Scott Turow from **"Innocent"**

In Oregon, some of the most beautiful days come in September and October. I have known Junes when it rained every single day or seemed to and it is generally expected to rain on the 4th of July. (Cranky old St. Swithin in faraway medieval England predicted that if it rained on the 15th of July, it would continue to rain for the following six weeks. That can be true for Western Oregon also).

But September and October can be glorious. After a brisk night and a cool morning, the sun will warm up to a sunny summer afternoon. There will not be a cloud in the sky and a soft ocean breeze will drift up the broad Columbia River to Portland. We will all delight in one more day of beauty before the winter rains.

On such an October day in 1940, my life turned completely around. The phone rang. Ben said, "I don't have to go to work until later tonight. I thought maybe we could spend the afternoon together and then have dinner. I'll get you out to work in good time." Work for Ben meant his position as a brakeman for the Oregon Electric Railway. For me...I was a chorus girl at Jack and Jill Elations Club, Portland's version of a big city night club.

"Oh Ben," I said, "I'd love to but I can't. I just washed my hair. It's up in curlers. I can't go out looking like this." And that was true. One didn't go out in public looking like a hedgehog in those days. We were much more formal then.

"Oh come on," he teased. "We can drive up into the west hills, up Barnes Road and out Skyline or Cornell Road. It's such a beautiful day. Nobody will see you and I can give you a driving lesson."

"But I don't want you to see me like this," I protested.

"Tie a rag around your head. It doesn't matter. You always look lovely to me."

Well, how could I refuse? I did as he suggested, tied the prettiest scarf I owned around my head and applied my make up very carefully to compensate. Then, I filled a bag with chocolate chip cookies to take along. Dancers are always hungry. As I sat on the porch swing waiting for Ben, I pondered our…what? Romance? Loving friendship?

Ben wasn't the only man I was seeing in those days but definitely the most important. I knew I liked him a lot but felt afraid to admit to myself just how much I cared for him. He was the nicest man I'd ever met. Now, "nice" might seem like a tame word meaning proper, dull, polite, or predictable but I'm using the word "nice" to tell about a man who was honest, reliable, gentle, considerate, intelligent, enthusiastic, people-oriented. He loved people and enjoyed himself as much, chatting with our neighbor's four-year old granddaughter as he did with his own 80-plus grandparents. He had a wealth of friends and had "never met a stranger." He possessed a wonderful sense of humor and also that magical, mysterious quality called charm or personality. The whole atmosphere changed, became more alive when he entered a room. Does this sound like maybe I was in love?

And, oh yes, he was good looking with curly black hair and brown eyes that really did twinkle and he had such a happy smile that you just had to smile along with him. We were so easy and comfortable together, almost reading each other's minds; finishing each other's sentences. And, on the romantic side, well, I needn't go into that. Suffice it to say, thank goodness we were both old-fashioned.

Yet Ben had never said those important three little words. In fact, he had never even asked me to "go steady" with him. Why hadn't he?

Maybe I wasn't being fair. I wanted him to "say something." If he did, I wouldn't be able to give him the answer he wanted.

Ever since my first dance class at the Alta Eastman Travis School of Dance at the age of eight, I *knew* I'd grow up to be a dancer. In those first lessons, the acrobatics scared me some but soon I took great pride in being able to do all these fantastic tricks. I liked tap dancing but I truly loved the classic ballet. Small, quick, and light, I learned the steps as though I had always known them. The music took possession of me and made me dance. Nobody had to tell me I had talent. I knew it in my bones.

I took lessons from Portland's best teachers. When my latest teacher, William F. Christenson, left Portland to become director of the San Francisco Opera Ballet, I wanted to follow as soon as I could afford it. But I knew the opera company paid only by the performances. The season lasted only six weeks of the year and not every opera included a ballet. The ballet company did give a few performances independently during the year but certainly not enough work to make a living. I had danced with the Christenson Ballet Company in Portland and with the San Francisco Ballet on tour but my goal included saving enough money to go to New York to continue training and find work with one of the fledgling companies that were springing up. But I also understood it would be hard to leave Portland now…to leave Ben.

His arrival put an end to my musings. When I got into the car, I started to say something about my hair in curlers. He stopped me saying, "Stop fussing. I've seen my mom in curlers. They're not important. I just had to come see you today. There's something I want to talk about."

Oh? We drove up Barnes Road and out Skyline Blvd. on this beautiful, glorious sunny afternoon. The trees glowed in all their many autumn colors. Looking down on the Tualatin Valley was like looking at a patchwork quilt. Some fields were green with pasture grass, some brown, plowed and ready for winter crops, and some with deep saffron shades of stubble after harvest. Patches of woodland offered a colorful mixture of dark green firs, golden oaks and flaming maples. A scene of such beauty; it still glows in my memory after more than 70 years.

We came to a place where Ben could pull off the road. He announced that he was serious about the driving lesson. I felt petrified, probably the only woman in the country who did not want to learn to drive. Machines of any kind always take an instant dislike to me and do all they can to make me look stupid. But wanting to be a good sport and praying that I wouldn't disgrace myself too badly, I took my place behind the wheel. Driver's seats didn't adjust in 1930s cars and a 5'2" person had to be propped up on cushions to see through the steering wheel with more cushions stuffed behind her back to be able to reach the pedals. At least I already knew how the stick shift worked. How else could Ben drive with an arm around me unless I could shift for him as he worked the clutch?

Working the clutch and gas pedal in coordination with the stick shift took some skill, one I didn't find easy to acquire. The poor car lurched and bucked down the road. Skyline Blvd. was a narrow, winding two-lane road. I never dreamed that the steering wheel of a car would be so responsive to my lightest touch. A too sharp tug at that wheel as we went around a tight curve, and I couldn't find the brake, and we slid slowly and inevitably into the ditch!

Ben got out immediately and inspected everything. No damage to the car, I'd only been going about five miles an hour. Nobody got hurt but I could have died! Ben acted so sweet and calm. "Not to worry. Anything can be fixed."

He tried to push the car out of the ditch. (He was the strongest man I've ever known). The car wouldn't budge. Skyline Blvd. and Cornell Road were lonely country roads. We hadn't seen another car in all the time we'd been up there. We'd have to walk to the nearest farm house to call for help. I couldn't even remember seeing a house. I repeat, I could have died.

Ben got back in the car, took me in his arms and said, "I love you. Will you marry me?"

"Wha—at?"

"I love you," he repeated. "Will you marry me? Here…" and he thrust a small blue velvet box into my hands. I opened it and there shone the most beautiful engagement ring…exactly the ring I'd have chosen myself.

"Wait a minute," I said, feeling perhaps just a little taken for granted. "You bought this ring without ever saying anything to me. How did you know…I would…I mean, what made you think…"

"Well, you had to love me back," he said, "because I love you so much. Do you?"

And there I am, sitting there with my hair in curlers. I've just put his car in the ditch and he wants to marry me. Of course, I admitted that I loved him but the ring still sat in the box. I looked at it, sparkling there in the sunlight, and in one brief moment, I saw a ballet studio, white tutus and satin toe shoes. I saw a stage and felt myself standing, scared, in the wings, watching the orchestra in the dark theater…with here and there the gleam of a white shirt front or a reflection of light from someone's glasses. I felt the sense of oneness with the other dancers as we moved together, taking the audience with us to a place of beauty, light, color and movement. Oh the joy of becoming part of the glorious music.

But Ben was holding me. I felt his nearness and dearness, and I knew that the only place I wanted to be for the rest of my life was in his arms. I was home. I let him slip the ring on my finger.

In the middle of a long and tender embrace we heard a "clop, clop, clop" behind us. We quickly broke apart and looked out the back window. A man on a big, black horse came riding up the road toward us.

"Need a little help?" He asked as he came alongside.

"Sure do," Ben replied getting out of the car. "I've got a rope in the trunk." I would find through the years that Ben always had the rope or tool or piece of lumber that the situation called for.

The two men, though perfect strangers, both farm-raised and animal-wise, worked together almost without words and soon had everything rigged up. The horse seemed knowledgeable about her part too. She pulled with all her strength. Ben pushed with all his might, and I steered and prayed with all my soul, and the car eased back up onto the road.

We thanked the man profusely. We couldn't believe our luck that he came riding to our rescue on such a lonely road. He told us he rode this way every Saturday afternoon and was glad he could be of help. Ben offered to pay him something, but of course, he refused.

I couldn't restrain myself. "Look," I said, waving my left hand in front of his face. "We just got engaged!"

"Well, congratulations," he replied. "No, I won't take any money for helping a person out but I will take a kiss from the young lady who just got engaged."

I gave him a nice smooch on the cheek. He and Ben shook hands. We both patted that beautiful black horse and told her what a jewel she was. Just like in old Westerns, the man tipped his hat and rode away.

And, that was the day that changed my life. I would always dance for the sheer pleasure of it, but from now on, the love of my life would be Ben, my beloved.

11

"The Question"

**By
Robb Bokich**

[**EDITOR'S NOTE**: *Robb Bokich planned on being a mechanical engineer then the crash changed his direction to counseling. He completed his Masters degree, but paid for it and ended up supporting himself with a self employed business which used his engineering skills to develop and maintain. He had the opportunity to travel as part of his personal rehabilitation. It helped him develop both his body and the strength to take care of himself.]*

* * *

"Could you write it?" The words came anxiously from my father's mouth as he stood to respond to the first sounds he had heard from me in over two and a half months.

My sister, Nancy Ann, laughed as Kathy who was driving us for a vacation in Eugene, Oregon joked with her about all the boys she might meet while there. The social life was of no interest to me as I was focused on the outdoors; beautiful lakes, trees, hiking and boating.

The doctors had told my family I would never come out of the coma, so when my eyes opened and the sounds I made were painful guttural noises my father was both shocked and concerned. His first question came in the same breath as his movement toward me, "What's wrong Robb what's wrong?"

Cars whizzed by us on the McKenzie highway. It had been a beautiful drive in the sun through the High desert in Idaho and then into the mountains of Oregon, and now as the sun set Nancy Ann fell asleep in the front seat. I moved some luggage to lie down in the back. I closed my eyes and listened to the sounds of cars and tires dreaming of the adventure to come.

Suddenly Kathy screamed as an oncoming speeding car pulled into our lane headed directly for us. She quickly responded jerking the wheel left to try and avoid the collision. The car was already on us, so the jerk avoided the head on collision, but couldn't stop the explosion of the force from their right headlight meeting our right head light in a combined speed collision of over 100 miles an hour!

The force threw my sister through the windshield leaving her mangled body crushed on the highway.

Nancy Ann was a beautiful girl. At age fourteen she had already danced in the Swan Lake ballet with the Boise

Philharmonic Orchestra. I have fond memories of getting to throw her around the living room when she practiced her jumps. She was a special person to her friends. They expressed great loss both of her friendship and of her personal support for their lives. She did not wake only went to sleep with a smile and laughter on her lips.

There were no seat belts in 1967, so Kathy was also affected. She was very short, less than five feet tall, so instead of going over the steering wheel, her lower weight was sent under the wheel throwing her whole body, feet first into the foot board. The force pushed her feet to her hips crushing her legs, and leaving her in pain to watch the injuries to Nancy Ann and me.

I was in the back seat asleep, and as the car jerked violently sideways, it threw my body head first into the window knob. The knob entered the right side of my head crushing my brain, and the handle connected to the knob followed crushing more of my skull.

So now I lay in pools of blood in a mangled car a little more than 60 miles from Eugene.

Someone called 911, but it took the ambulance longer than an hour to arrive, even longer to assess the situation and gain access to my body. They finally reached me, cut a hole for a tracheotomy, and then another hour to drive to Eugene to get me on the operating table.

During the drive three major blood clots had formed on the left side of my head, so the first thing the doctors did was drill three more holes to remove blood and relieve pressure on my brain. Next, they removed broken pieces of skull and replaced it with a kind of liquid plastic to fill and protect the hole. Now, riddled with holes and deep in a coma, doctors moved me to the third floor critical care unit.

Nurses gathered around my bed to help calm and support. My only response to dad's first question was more pained noises. Dad looked up at the nurses hoping for an answer. The nurses stood also bewildered that I was making any sounds at all. They knew I had become a hemiplegic. Complete paralysis of my left side.

With body loss from the right side brain damage and my face, throat, lips, and tongue from the blood clots on my left side, so after the paralization of my face, throat, lips and tongue from blood clots any response from me surprised everyone.

With pained guttural sounds ; everyone just stood and stared. Suddenly my father had an incredible thought, and asked 'the question,' "Could you write it?" I nodded yes, and a nurse practically leaped over with a pad and pen. The room went silent except for the beeping sounds from the machines keeping me alive. A nurse held the pad so I could write with my good hand, "what are the tubes for?"

My father stuttered, stunned both from the joy of communication and from not knowing how to answer. He just said, "I don't know."

I motioned for the pad and wrote, "Ask Mrs. Nelson."

Kathy Nelson, the daughter of our family friends, the Nelsons, drove the car, and her mom was with her at that time, so my dad still stumbling over words said, "Mrs. Nelson is very far from here, I can't get her right now."

To this my response became even more amazing as I pointed up at a nurse. My dad looked over, and there on her name tag was the name 'Mrs. Nelson'.

I'm near sighted, and they wouldn't have me wearing my glasses while I was in the coma, so the only time I could have seen a name tag would have been when the nurses were helping or working on me. With the realization I was so aware; the medical staff began to prepare me to come out of the coma.

Coming out of a coma is not like they show on TV. It usually takes one to three weeks. After about a week, I began to be able to say my first word with a very airy, "Haaaa" (that's Hi). And soon after that I doubled my vocabulary with more air and, "Hu Aaa (that's Goodbye). My speech now is pretty good. My joke about my speech is, 'My speech is so good, only my speech therapist knows for sure.'

The crash took place during the July 1st 1967 Fourth of July Holiday. It was caused by a drunk driver who killed himself and his wife.

I am now 62, traveled around the world a year and a half after the crash, and have to dedicate my life and success to both my father and my mother for all their love and support.

* * *

"The Fall "

Tension and anxiety filled my head as I prepared to leave Afghanistan and travel to Iran, the next stop on my world tour. My departure became so difficult it was almost cancelled except for a major fall.

It all started in 1963. I was in the 6th grade. School had ended for the day. I wasn't excited about the mile and a half walk home only to have to feed the chickens and clean the barn, so I decided to stay and play with friends. We were running outside the school fence when Rick called my name. I turned and darted toward him, but was stopped abruptly when I tripped on something, throwing me down hard on my knees, followed quickly by a long ripping sound, filling my ears with fright! I had torn my good school pants, and mom was going to kill me!

As I got up trying to figure out what to do , I looked down at my right knee to see the damage to my pants, and let out a scream as my eyes filled with tears. True, a delayed reaction, but still appropriate for the sight before me. From the large hole torn in my pants blood spewed out drenching my leg in red! I had fallen on a board with a nail sticking up. The nail had gone a full two inches into my leg tearing a three inch gash beside my knee cap. With my friend's help I hobbled back to the school where they cleaned and stitched me back together. The wound healed in time leaving me with a large scar on my right knee.

Now, seven years later, I'm nineteen years old, and traveling in Afghanistan.

Trying to make the most of my last days in Afghanistan, I trucked out to a neighboring village to spend the day visiting with the people, looking at how the mud houses were built, walking with the cows, and enjoying the food. I had delicious rice and vegetables, and of course my favorite, the handmade ice cream.

This simple meal fit the lives of the Afghanistan people in this village. The walls of their houses were straight caked mud and the kitchen consisted of a piece of metal with a bowl shape at one end for the sink, and a waved area on the other end to act like a drain.

I finished my dinner with two extra orders of ice cream, and being tired, got ready to return to where I was staying in Kabul. Travel in this area was done mainly on big flatbed trucks. The drivers took great pride in their trucks and spent many hours cleaning and decorating with colorful ribbons and ornaments; always a delight to see the trucks before climbing on. This truck today had red ribbons everywhere and a driver adorned in a red shirt. He and his friends recognized I was crippled and quickly came to help me climb up on to the back of the truck to join the crowd of a couple of dozen people, pigs and poultry. I smiled at the people beside me and relaxed for the ride to Kabul.

The smells of manure and sweat were strong and the tight space uncomfortable but in my exhausted state, I had no trouble falling asleep leaning against the side of the truck. Unfortunately these tight quarters also provided the opportunity to steal.

While I slept, someone carefully slipped their hand down my shirt into my security neck pouch and slipped out my passport leaving me to sleep and discover its disappearance later. The next morning in Kabul, I reached into my pouch to pay for breakfast and made the shocking discovery, my passport was gone. I was in trouble. The missing passport created a big problem in my leaving the country and I sat stunned trying to think. I felt like a giant weight had been placed on my back. I really didn't know what to do.

After a while I decided my first step should be to go to the American Embassy. Hopefully they would have the answers to the many questions racing through my head.

I found the address at the hotel desk, along with general directions and left with the mission before me. As I walked I watched for the American flag. Step clomp, step clomp. The brace on my leg felt like a sack of bricks added to the weight on my back.

I walked about a half mile and finally saw the flag above the buildings about three blocks away. One final turn and I arrived at the doorsteps of a very large and gleaming white building. The giant door towered over my crippled body and I felt weak as I struggled to pull open the heavy door.

Inside more shine from the floor and a pleasant greeting from a young woman behind a desk asking how she could help me. Wow! I thought. A conversation in English! It had been over a month since I had talked to another American and in this beautiful building I felt able to relax a little. I excitedly began to tell her of my long ride on the truck the day before and how my passport had been stolen. She interrupted me mid-story, got my name and asked me to sit and wait. Huh! Not quite the response I expected. I walked over to the waiting area and found a place to sit. In the firm giant lounge chair I felt like a school kid in trouble waiting to see the principal.

I sat fidgeting and after a long wait an embassy officer wearing a sharp black suit and tie finally came out and called my name. I quickly began to speak, but he waved his hand to silence me and ushered me down the long hallway to his office. Step, clomp, step, clomp my legs tensed, and I thought to myself, "This isn't going to be easy!"

In his office he asked me to sit and tell him the problem. I again began to explain the story of how my passport had been stolen and how important it was to get a new one as soon as possible because I was getting ready to leave Afghanistan. He, in a very formal voice, just asked me for a picture i.d. I explained I had none except for my passport. He responded calmly, "Without a picture i.d. I can't give you a new passport."

My voice began to quiver as my tension turned to fear, "What can I do?" The officer now began to explain we could send away for a picture i.d., but it usually took three to six weeks. He did say he could start the process immediately if I wanted.

I sat in silence trying to think. The reality of my situation overwhelming me, and the embassy officer offered no real hope. Then in a more flustered state I put my hand inside my shirt to dig in my neck pouch searching for an answer. I picked through some papers and money in my pouch and pulled out my social security card. I felt I had a glimmer of hope. I showed him the card with my name and number on it saying, "That's me!" He looked at the card and then at me and said simply, "This only proves you have a card with Robb Bokich's name on it. Not enough for a passport."

I stuttered for a moment and then remembered my social security card had descriptive information on the back. I read it to him. It said I have a tracheotomy scar on my neck and I pulled back my shirt to show him the round scar. I also told him a little about the car crash I was in at age 16. I thought any kind of sympathy I could get right now would be valuable.

I sat waiting for the good news. He looked at the scar and said almost sadly, "Lots of people have a trach scar. Sorry still not enough." I drew back even more flustered but pressed on. It also says I have a long scar on my right knee. I handed him the card so he could see the words as I jerked my pant leg up above my knee and there it was! A long scar. I lifted my leg putting it closer to his face. I went on to explain the logic that a lot of people might have a trach scar but to have a trach scar and a long scar on the right knee is extremely unique. At this point the embassy officer stood smiling, offered his hand and said, "I'm convinced you are you." I wanted to jump up and give him a hug but thought getting a smile out of him was reward enough. I shook his hand and thanked him.

He then went on to say, "We'll arrange for your new passport immediately." If I could have skipped I would have out of his office. I returned to my small rented room and packed my few belongings to prepare to leave for Iran. Beaming with joy, I climbed on the plane the next day happy to be leaving Afghanistan and continuing on with my adventure.

* * *

"Next Stop Hungary"

Budapest, Hungary. Just saying the name of the capital city was exciting to me. I was sorry to leave Yugoslavia but excited to go deeper into communist controlled Europe.

In keeping with my different modes of travel hobby I decided to fly Hungarian Airlines. I arranged my flight, bought my ticket and planned my travel time to the airport. I arrived at the airport with great excitement and walked to the boarding gate. Step clomp step clomp.

I couldn't read the names, but knew the flight number. At the gate, I sat to wait and began talking with the people around me, No English, but my sign language was very successful. The woman with two children beside me had just gone to Yugoslavia to visit their Grandmother. They had a good visit, and the children were very excited to tell me all about it! I didn't understand a word, but the smile and occasional nod told them easily how much I enjoyed their stories.

The airline woman behind the desk made an announcement, and people stood to walk to the door. Time to board the plane. As I walked I looked up and my enthusiasm was quickly quelled. After flying all the big jets with all the main airlines it looked funny to see this little 20 person twin propeller plane. The coloring was a drab grey, but it had wings and wheels so I continued walking thinking "What could happen?"

I struggled up the steep steps; step lift clomp, step lift clomp and at the top stepped inside the small door. I found my seat number and got settled greeting the person beside me with a smile. He also did not speak English, but did say "Hi" with a smile.

We prepared for takeoff. The instructions were all in Hungarian, but I could tell when the stewardess held up the belt she meant for us to buckle ourselves in. We paused on the runway for a few minutes while I looked out the small window checking out the flat terrain and airport workers waving their lights at the pilot to signal us to start. The propellers began to turn.

 You could tell the propellers had to get up to a certain speed because we sat waiting as the sound of the spinning wings went higher and higher. All I could see from the windows was a whirling blur.

I began to relax a little as the plane finally started down the runway picking up speed faster and faster. I was all ready to watch the ground disappear at the end of the runway, when suddenly the engines shut down. I thought, 'This is weird, never considered this possibility.' No announcements just continued motion as we taxied back ready to try again. I'd never heard of a plane not getting up except in a crash. I did not like the sound of my own thoughts

We sat waiting for signals. The ground people waved their wands, and the propellers were again given power. Down the runway we raced again; this time for sure! I listened to the sound of the propellers getting higher and higher, louder and louder then suddenly quiet as the engines shut down right before the end of the concrete.

Back into taxi mode as we traveled slowly back to the starting line. All comfort and relaxed feelings had disappeared as my only thoughts were trying to figure out how to get off the plane, but couldn't ask in Hungarian or even find out what was happening. OK, now I'm hanging tightly onto my seat sweat creeping down my face; the plane had taxied back to the starting line once more for try number three. This time I'll hold my breath to make the plane lighter, and pull up on my seat. One more time down the runway faster and faster. All I could think of was, 'Don't crash don't crash!'

Then it happened. We left the ground! I kept checking to see if it was an optical illusion, but no, we were really airborne. I was still very tense and frustrated that I couldn't talk with anyone, so I just sat alone in fear. Finally after about an hour of smooth flying I was relaxed enough to stand and go to the bathroom.

As I stood I lost my balance because my legs were still weak so I stood holding the back of the seat beside me until I felt stable enough to walk. Step clomp step clomp. I stepped into the bathroom closing the door behind me. Click lock. I turned, unzipped my pants, and stabilized myself as best I could with my right elbow.

I began to pee. Oh, what a relief.

Suddenly the toilet was beside me and the sink before me, as the plane had tipped on its side throwing me against the wall! I was like a toppled statue of David peeing all over the room. From the speakers in the main room I could hear the loud squabble of Hungarian voices. It was loud and it was frantic, so I wasted no time struggling to stand to get back to a seat. Of course the lock did not function smoothly or my fingers were so tight it took what seemed like forever to get it open. Once it opened, I grabbed the first available seat and buckled myself in. I then took care of the minor detail of putting myself back in and zipping up.

No sleep for me on this flight. We did finally land, and I felt like kissing the ground! Walking into the terminal in

Hungary I thought I could relax for the evening, but the border guard had a different idea. As I approached the entry gate he greeted me with the question, "What are you doing here?" I answered simply, "I'm coming to visit Hungary." His next statement basically vetoed that idea; without a thought he told me, "You can't come here."

It turned out that Hungary being a strictly controlled communist country did not allow just anybody into the country. You needed special arrangements, escorts, money and or credentials. I had few of these or should I say none of these. What I did have was hair down past my shoulders, and an airline ticket that cost me less than a dollar that gave me entry into three communist controlled countries.

At that point I told the guard I didn't have plans on leaving soon, and if they were going to send me somewhere I would not climb on that plane again. I was already there, I walked into Hungary, and enjoyed my stay. Step clomp, step clomp.

12

"An Unexpected Treasure"

By
Corinne Grosenick

[EDITOR'S NOTE: *Corinne Anderson Grosenick and husband Conrad migrated to Oregon for retirement in 1999. Born in Chicago, Corrine graduated from St. Mary-of-the-Woods College in Indiana. She and Conrad have three children, Kip, Kitty, and Kendall, who live in Atlanta, Denver, and Portland.*]

* * *

Early in the year of 2000, Conrad, and I attended a cruise workshop at Willamalane Senior Center. We had never taken a cruise before, but when a travel agent totaled up the value of a cruise: lodging, meals, entertainment, and other amenities, my husband loved the idea. Especially interested in a Holland America cruise "Gems of the Baltic" including Stockholm, St. Petersburg and Helsinki, we realized we actually could afford it! Seeing our keen interest, the travel agent called us later saying free airfare was now available in order to fill the trip. We signed up immediately!

Both my father's parents came from Sweden so I was really pleased with our destination. Almost as an afterthought, I remembered that I had a list of Swedish "cousins." (One of my aunts provided the list several years ago, saying maybe we would use it someday). With great anticipation I sent each one a form letter saying we planned a July visit to Sweden asking if they could tell me anything about my family's history.

Sending seven letters--two came back with "deceased" and "no one at this address." One also came telling me, in a quivering hand, that both persons in the couple were elderly and not well, and had lost track of most of the original Anderson family members.

Then one bright day in June, Gunnel and Lennart Johnsson sent a welcome e-mail from Alem, Sweden. In English, Gunnel told me that Lennart's grandmother and my grandmother were sisters. Gunnel said she taught school, Lennart retired from farming, and they would love to have us come for a visit in July. She said their son, Frans, was getting married on July 15, in the village where they lived. But we could come the week before or the day after the wedding. Since we had reservations in New York City the week before, we agreed to July 16. We made arrangements to take the train south to Kalmar when we arrived in Stockholm. You can imagine the excitement we felt on that train trip from Stockholm to Kalmar where Lennart and Gunnel were waiting for us!

In preparation, I sent ahead a snapshot of the two of us. But when we stepped off the train we wondered how we would recognize them! It was not difficult--there they were running toward us. Both had broad smiles! She was small and wiry. He, a bit older than she, was slower and stocky. They grabbed our hands, hugged us, and kept smiling. Both Conrad and I immediately felt their warmth and eagerness to make us feel welcome.

We turned and walked toward their car, a Volvo, of course. Gunnel just kept talking, "Were we tired? Hungry? Was it a good trip?" Lennart seemed to be listening intently. We drove quite a ways through a densely wooded area, arriving in the small town of Alem where my grandmother lived before coming to America in 1896.

The biggest surprise came pulling into a long circular drive leading to a huge frame house that we later learned was over 250 years old. As we watched, a young man came out and propped open the front door. Gunnell said, "There is Frans, our son, opening our house to welcome you!"

And so began one of the most unforgettable experiences of our lives. Never have we been treated so royally! We still remember the warm greeting of Frans and his new wife Ulrika as we entered, as Gunnel said, "Welcome to our home!" The next two days were filled with conversation and much laughter. They took us to the church where my grandmother was confirmed, to an open field where her family's house once stood, and to an old-fashioned cemetery where there were gravestones marking many of my ancestors.

The second day, we visited the crystal factory "Orrefors" and Castle Fjord in Kalmar, the only preserved Renaissance castle in Sweden surrounded by a moat and open to the public as a museum. We ate lunch in a nearby open-air restaurant in the summer sunshine. Gunnel told us all Swedes like to spend as much time as possible outdoors and in the sun in the summertime.

That afternoon, we returned to the homestead where Frans and Ulrika had prepared afternoon coffee for us. It was set out on a coffee table covered with a lace tablecloth and the best china and crystal, plus many sweet things served along with Gelvalia coffee. (Did I tell you that Frans and Ulrika had postponed their honeymoon to meet "the American cousins"?) We complimented them on the beautiful table and their hospitality. Our conversation then focused on their rituals and customs. In turn, they asked…"What are *your* customs? Tell us how *you* do things in America."

We presented gifts for the family: USA 2,000 tee-shirts for everyone, even one for the daughter working in Stockholm, Anna-Carin, Marionberry jam, and two copies of my Anderson family cookbook. Gunnel and Ulrika looked up my recipe for rice pudding and compared it to their recipe. (Later, Gunnel wrote to say Anna-Carin wore her tee-shirt to work and received much attention for it).

Hours later there was a big dinner with delicious fresh fish fried hot and crispy followed by a huge rice pudding, the best I've ever tasted. We were joined by another uncle and his daughter who did not speak English, but they nodded and smiled, and listened to our conversation. We stayed up quite late looking at photographs, the family history they had prepared, and discussing our extended family.

The next morning, our last, they were up with breakfast ready for us when we came downstairs. Breakfast was a beautifully arranged platter of meat and cheese. They also served cereal with liquid yogurt poured from a carton. Coffee, of course, rich and strong. I never saw them do dishes or prepare the meals, everything just appeared miraculously. Gunnel was a bundle of energy and a wonderful hostess. They drove us to the train station that morning so we could return to the Stockholm airport. They seemed a little sad and wistful as we were leaving and I have a picture I took of them outside the train window, waving and smiling. Before we left,

Gunnel said, "I want to thank you for this visit. It was a wonderful opportunity to practice my English." (She was fluent in English, as were Frans and Ulrika.) Children in Sweden, Gunnel said, begin their language study in the lower grades and are proficient in English by the 8th grade.

Since then, we have exchanged many letters and e-mails. Gunnel is very busy during the school year; and finds time to correspond only on holidays and in the summer. Last year, she wrote me asking if I could help her make a contact for pen-pals for her fifth grade class. I was able to do so with Oaklea Middle-School in Junction City. On her Christmas card Gunnel wrote that the pen-pal program was going well and she would tell me more about it later.

What a great experience! I feel very fortunate to have met these wonderful people--my Swedish cousins--an unexpected treasure!

Footnote: Unfortunately, soon after our visit, Lennart went into the hospital for surgery and later was put on dialysis. In 2007, he passed away. Gunnel and I still correspond. We exchange pictures of grandchildren and news of our families, but I am so glad we made that visit in 2000 and that I met my cousin, Lennart Johnsson.

* * *

"Why Are We Here…"

It happened again just recently,
I saw her at Safeway last week,
checking out, with another woman
Her caregiver paid, they left together.
But when she looked my way,
There was no hint of recognition

No recognition was the same clue

Seeing another old friend yesterday
Someone I knew just last year.
She had been in my home,
But now she didn't know me,
Her eyes vacant, the sparkle gone.

Where is the sparkle of life?
What gives our life its meaning?
I begin to see what matters
Our lives are relatively short
When some lose their independence
We wonder at our very existence.

Our own existence here is brief
Make the most of our time
Love one another, love and laugh
Make friends, forgive one another
Don't let the days pass without
Sharing the wealth of good feelings.

Good feelings abound if we share
What we know, learning from others
Treasuring days even as they pass
Someday, we too, will be helpless,
Letting someone else care for us
Not recognizing those we once knew.

Hoping friends remember us warmly
As we end this earthly life
Knowing we loved, laughed, lived well.

* * *

"Our Evans Scholar"

When our 15 year-old son, Kip, applied for a job at the Fort Wayne Country Club Restaurant, Phil Antibus interviewed him. Recognizing a good student, Phil encouraged him to caddy instead. If he did, he might be eligible for a four-year college scholarship. That summer, Kip attended the country club orientation for caddies. None of us knew then how hard those caddies work!

A caddy master assigns caddies to specific golfers. Beginning caddies are rated "C." Gaining experience, they move up to "B," and with extra effort—they become "A" caddies. As experienced caddies, they are assigned to serious golfers who prefer having a regular caddy. This relationship profits both the golfer and the caddy. Kip sometimes came home with $50-$70 in his pocket as well as being sunburned sweaty and exhausted. A hard worker, he never talked about quitting. Kip saved most of his money for college, although he did buy a color TV for his room the second summer.

In 1980 after three summers of caddying and excellent grades in high school, Kip received the Fort Wayne Country Club Caddy Scholarship. This provided room, board, tuition, books and fees at Kip's choice of Indiana University, in Bloomington, IN. The scholars live in a house on fraternity row called the Evans House. They have a reputation for high academic standards on campus, but with time for a social life too. Kip told us about a party they held for the sorority girls, where one girl asked him incredulously, "You mean you're all *caddies*?"

Evans scholars earned their evening meal at Chi Omega, a sorority just up the hill. The boys worked in the kitchen or dining room and then ate dinner. Kip volunteered to do pots and pans. I thought he might like to be in the dining room where the girls were. But when I asked, he told me that wasn't for him. "Those girls are too hard to please, often sending waiters back to the kitchen, not once, but many times, with special requests." He said he preferred to finish early with the pots and pans, eat dinner and return to the Evans House to concentrate on his homework. And he added, "...my fingernails are always clean."

Evans Scholars, the brain child of golfer Chick (Charles) Evans, the first amateur to win the U.S. Open and U.S. Amateur in 1916, began as a caddy at the Edgewater Golf Club in Chicago. He went on to become one of the most acclaimed golfers of his time, earning a spot in the World Hall of Golf Fame in 1975. Chick dedicated himself to making college available for middle class young people by establishing caddy scholarships at many golf courses in the Illinois and Indiana area. In 1930, the Evans Scholars Foundation was formed.

The criteria used to choose recipients were caddy experience, excellent grades, character and financial need. Over 9,600 caddies have become Evans Scholars and completed college educations. There are now 14 Evans Scholar Houses on state campuses across the country. Chick Evans died in 1979, but his goals live on. Today it is the largest privately-funded sports scholarship program in the United States.

Our son, Kip, completed his education in 1985 with a double major of English and Tele-Communications, graduating with honors from Indiana University. While in college, he held positions as secretary and vice-president of his Evans chapter and made life-long friendships.

Kip's first job was with CNN in Atlanta, signing on as a video journalist in 1985 and progressing to the position of senior producer. After seventeen years, he left CNN to form his own company, Robin Hood Productions, free-lancing at ABC, CBS, Fox News, and the Weather Channel. His areas of expertise include politics, NASCAR, and the environment. He holds a second-degree black belt in Cuong Nhu. He and his wife, Michell, and children, Shelby and Spencer, live in Avondale Estates, just outside of Atlanta.

13

"My Children's Grandfather"

By
Susan Rogers

[**EDITOR'S NOTE**: *Susan Rogers: Lifelong writer since early childhood. Human Resources Analyst, Los Angeles County; Program Analyst, State of California Licensing 1960's - 1998. Oregon Licensed Massage Therapist since 2004. Marathon walker, garlic grower, snail rescuer, now revisiting past life events, interests and ordeals to create my memoir.*]

* * *

From my childhood through my adult life, I often struggled with my hope to maintain a loving and respectful relationship with my father. His desire to control the life choices of his family members caused some irresolvable conflicts, so perhaps it should not have been surprising that he left a painful and puzzling legacy when he died.

My father, a Eugene resident for almost 60 years, passed away in 1990 at age 88 after suffering a stroke. My four children and I came from California to handle the funeral arrangements and to support my 89 year old mother through the process. As our family gathered together that week in my father's world that had not always included us, our thoughts turned to our mixed feelings at his death.

A hard working man focused on his career, my dad was well known throughout Oregon for his accomplishments in city planning, research, and establishment of state civil service and retirement systems. I appreciated his values, his strong sense of responsibility, his love of the outdoors, and compassion for animals, but in our family life, he was the domineering boss of the household, often controlling and critical.

Looking back into the past, I know that from the beginning, my life did not meet the expectations my father may have envisioned for his children. Prior to my birth as a baby girl, my intended name was Steven Eugene Kenzli, although I did not know until later of my father's bitter lifelong disappointment in failing to have a son. Although I was an excellent student, I was perceived as a shy quiet child, and my father instructed me to be more "aggressive."

Accidentally pregnant and deserted by my boyfriend shortly after my college graduation, I fled to Colorado for graduate school to conceal my pregnancy in 1959. When I eventually told my parents that I was an unmarried mother with an infant daughter, my parents visited us in Colorado, but my father made it clear that I was no longer welcome in Eugene.

Since I grew up in Eugene with a 99 percent white population, it certainly never occurred to me that I would marry someone who was not white. But in Denver, I worked at a large agency whose staff reflected the ethnic diversity of the city. I became friends with a large group of co-workers who were white, African American, Asian and Latino, and met for lunch in a park across the street from the office. Although my father taught me to be open minded and unbiased, when he learned that I was dating an African American man, he exploded, "All black men are drug addicts!"

In spite of his desperate efforts to break up our relationship, eventually Bill and I married and had three bi-racial children. My parents still visited us, but our relationship with my father became more strained as he displayed his racial biases. My parents had developed a loving relationship with my oldest daughter Joyce who is white. Since she is six to twelve years older than the younger biracial children, it wasn't immediately clear whether my parents would ultimately treat all four children equally.

As the years went by, my parents sent birthday and Christmas presents to all the children but they had not created a genuine bond with the younger ones. Not wanting to punish Joyce for my father's racism, we allowed her to continue her relationship with my parents and after she turned 16 we let her make her own decisions about visits and contacts. At an early age, my younger children sensed their grandparents' rejection of them, not fooled by the obligatory gift rituals.

At the time of my father's death, my daughter Joyce worked at a San Francisco hospital as a nutritionist, and my three younger children were in college - two at UC Berkeley and one at UCLA. Joyce had visited in Eugene many times and had taken several short trips with my parents. Wayne and Lynne had never been to Eugene, and my youngest daughter Georgene had visited Eugene once with Joyce. After her visit, Georgene was further disillusioned, telling stories of my father's discomfort when she called him Grandpa, and only being taken to out of the way places where no one would see her. She cringed at some of my father's conversational efforts "I bet your dad's good at basketball. Doesn't he play basketball?"

Until 1990, the year of my father's death, I had not returned to Eugene since I left in 1959 to conceal my pregnancy.

My mother welcomed us warmly. Mother had always been very nice to my children, but when my parents visited us through the years, my father was always present, never leaving her alone with us. It always seemed clear that my father made the decisions about how to relate to my family. Now with my father gone, my mother seemed less restrained in her interactions with my children, talking and laughing with them.

We planned a private funeral service which would be attended by our close family members scheduled for Wednesday afternoon at the funeral home. It was decided that my father's longtime university colleagues would coordinate a public memorial service on Thursday on campus. Then there would be a private burial service on Friday for family members.

Although I had over 20 cousins, mostly all more than seven years older than me, and many aunts and uncles and other more distant relatives, my contact with them had been cut off after my unmarried pregnancy and subsequent interracial marriage.

As the years went by, I sometimes thought about my family's isolation from relatives I knew when I was growing up, but with four children, a full time job, a busy life, and also not knowing how racist my other relatives would be, I somehow never figured out an approach to deal with the situation.

Since we did not see my parents frequently, my husband and I tried not to emphasize the problem for our children. In the meantime, we had close relationships with my husband's family. His parents gave equal love and attention to all four of our children, and his siblings were always supportive of our interracial family.

My children and I, along with my sister and her family, attended my father's service at the funeral home on Wednesday. A minister led the open casket ceremony and my daughter Georgene sang a moving rendition of Amazing Grace.

When we returned to my mother's apartment, my children tried to sort out their feelings. It was difficult because my oldest daughter Joyce had always received genuine love and support from my father, while my younger children had felt rejected through the years, sensing that his gifts were a feeble attempt to mask his lack of enthusiasm for them. I tried to encourage them each to feel their own pain and understand that their siblings' pain might be different, hoping that my father's legacy would not divide my family.

The next day, on Thursday, someone drove us to the memorial service at Gerlinger Hall on the University of Oregon campus. When I was a child, my father's office had always been located on campus, and driving there reminded me how my ties to Eugene and Oregon had been severed for more than 30 years. Over 200 people arrived for the service, and my family assembled in a reserved front row of seats.

The master of ceremonies stepped to the podium to deliver his opening remarks. We had persuaded my daughter Georgene to sing again at this service and arranged for a pianist to accompany her. Looking at the program, I realized that I was not acquainted with any of the speakers sharing their memories of my father that afternoon. When the emcee announced that Alfred Kenzli's granddaughter, a junior at UCLA, would sing, the room became silent as Georgene walked to the podium. I did not turn to look at the crowd, but later Georgene told us that when she faced the audience she saw some looks of amazement, confusion, and disbelief as they saw a 19 year old bi-racial woman with tight braids who was supposedly a granddaughter of the man who was being honored.

Undaunted, Georgene sang an inspiring rendition of Amazing Grace and returned to her seat with the family. The service went on with five speakers recounting their experiences in municipal government with my father until his retirement 18 years earlier. As the service came to an end, people broke into small groups to chat. A number of people lined up to talk to my daughter Georgene, and a group gathered to speak to me, mostly people that I did not know. Everyone was courteous and friendly, some people remarking lightly that my father wasn't inclined to share information about his family and grandchildren.

Eventually a stout blonde woman approached me. "Honey, I'm so sorry," she said. She grabbed my hand. "I'm your cousin. I met you when you were a little girl." Her name was Lenore and it turned out she was my mother's second cousin. She explained that she was the longtime coordinator of the annual family picnic and that she compiled and updated family records used to distribute a history book to family members. She stood with her hands on her hips. "Your page, the Susan Kenzli page has always been blank," she said. "Every year at the picnic, I asked your father, 'Where does Susan live? Is she married? Does she have children?' He would never answer me and he wouldn't let your mother answer me either." She sighed heavily, "Look at your children, they are grown and we did not even know that they existed. I am so sorry." She hugged me tightly and asked for my address and phone number so we could keep in touch and she could finally fill out my page for the family records. Other extended family members gathered around, baffled at my father's cover up, talking to my children, inviting them for visits to Oregon. Eventually, Lenore tried to assemble me and my mother and my children for photos, rapidly snapping as many pictures of us as she could.

It was late afternoon, and people began to leave. In comparing notes, all of my children had encountered people who were surprised to learn that Alfred Kenzli had grandchildren. In our family, although we were well aware of his racial biases, we had no idea that none of his longtime close colleagues and associates knew that my children existed, or that he routinely refused to give information about me to our relatives. My son and daughters were stunned to learn of his complete denial of them.

The Register Guard article about his death referred to him as a longtime community activist with a major influence on state and county government, a great mentor who had an enormous impact on many people's public careers. An editorial praised him as one of Oregon's true visionaries and one of Eugene's treasured resources, a man of curiosity and warmth, commitment and humor.

As my children and I left the memorial service and prepared for the burial the next day, we pondered the public and the private faces of my father.

* * *

"Meditations and Surrender Of A Garlic Addict"

Today my body is a prisoner of garlic
The fumes and emissions are my aura
There is no escape from the presence

14

"The Hitchhikers"

By
Barbara de Ronden-Pos

[**EDITOR'S NOTE:** *Barbara de Ronden-Pos served as a secretary-bookkeeper for several years and a small business owner—tavern and building supply for ten years. She later did financial planning and Real Estate Sales for 30 years. She is also a wife, mother, and grandmother.*]

***

There's a pure white light
that shines from above.
It radiates warmth and
unconditional love!

No one can hide from
this all knowing light
as it searches for truth

to make all things right.

Its help is available,
We have but to ask,
No matter how large
Or small is our task.

And with that help,
the world becomes brighter
for every load shared
becomes much lighter.

***

My parents divorced when I was seven. We lived in North Bend, Oregon at that time. It seems as though we lived there for a while so this incident had to have taken place prior to that time. My guess is that I was around the age of five or six at most.

My understanding is we lived in Bandon, Oregon and were driving to North Bend to visit and no doubt have Sunday dinner with my grandparents on mother's side. A marvelous cook and baker, Grandmother began baking bread for her family at the age of ten. Everyone looked forward to having any meal at Grandma's house.

Although not terribly far as the crow flies, the trip no doubt took much longer at that time. No freeways, only two narrow lanes and maybe shoulders on part of the roads. I can remember thinking how narrow the highway seemed as my dad and I stood beside the road. You could easily feel the breezes from any passing cars, although in truth, very few passed before we were offered a ride.

And how did we come to be standing beside the road? Well, I innocently asked my dad why there were people, especially soldiers, standing alongside the road with their thumbs up; a fairly common sight at the time—in the early 40's--war time.

He explained, "They need a ride to get somewhere—back home, back to camp. Many people were kind enough to stop and give them rides."

Apparently, he thought a lesson could be taught here as just minutes later, he stopped the car and told my mother to drive on to Grandma's house. He and I got out of the car and stood beside the road with our thumbs up! I felt pretty strange as I watched mother drive away, but I felt more curious than afraid because dad was with me.

It really didn't seem very long before a kindly couple stopped and asked if we needed a ride. Of course, we did! Why else would we be standing beside the road with our "thumbs up?" We climbed into their back seat, and as they queried us and heard the story, they decided to take us a few miles past their actual destination and right to Grandma's door!

Lesson accomplished!

Writing this down in 2013, I believe he most certainly would not do the same thing today. There are undoubtedly many good people still out there today just as there were at that time, but the question now is, who might stop in between?

* * *

"Grandma's Kitchen"

The simple, country-style square room kitchen featured a door entering from the screened in porch in the south wall. It also had a door into Grandma's bedroom and an opening to the stairwell in the east wall. The exterior west wall was lined with painted white cupboards over linoleum countertops and a single large sink under the window. I don't remember a refrigerator or an ice box, but perhaps there was. There were screened air vents from the outside in the cupboard next to the window over the sink. The oblong wooden table and chairs sat in the middle of the room. The large cast iron wood stove complete with warming oven took up most of the wall next to the living room. You could often find one or both small dogs sleeping behind it.

My parents divorced when I was about seven. Mother and I had come to live with her parents, her grandmother, and her youngest brother, who was in high school at the time. It was a small house for that many people. Two attic style bedrooms were upstairs, and mother and I and our dog slept in one. Her brother, my uncle, slept in the other.   Grandma and Grandpa had the bedroom downstairs off the kitchen and Great Grandma slept in a small room, almost like a large closet, off the living room. We all used the one bathroom downstairs between those two sleeping areas.

The house sat on a larger lot than most homes have today. With the lack of modern day deed restrictions, they kept chickens, rabbits, the two dogs, and a "barn" cat, or perhaps I should say a garage or shed cat since no barn existed.   I don't ever remember the cat being indoors. In those days they earned their room and board by being good "mousers". The small dogs, however, did nothing I can remember to earn their place in the family, much as it is to this day.

The grandparents also had a large "victory" garden. Among the abundant produce were peas so sweet I pulled them from the vine and ate them on the spot, or pulled up a carrot and washed it under the outside faucet. All in all, the grandparents were close to self sufficient. Of course, what wasn't eaten at the time was "canned" for later use. Nothing was wasted. If the cream went sour, she baked sour cream cookies. With all that and her wonderful cooking, we were more fortunate than many during that war time period in the 1940's.

Grandma could have been the role model for the original "energizer bunny", with all she managed to do in a day. She was actually a fairly small woman but did have a bit of extra girth about her middle. Perhaps having birthed and raised seven children had something to do with that.

Always up early, she began her day by brushing out the night time braid of her gray/blond hair and putting it in a bun for the day.

I always think of her in gingham plaid dresses with an apron over top, and black lace up shoes with a slight heel. She did have some special dresses which she referred to as, her "Sunday go to Meeting" outfits. She always wore a hat and carried or wore her coat. Grandpa wore a dark suit with a vest, complete with watch and chain, and always a felt hat with brim.

I usually went with them, wearing my best dresses as well. In those days girls only wore dresses whether to school or elsewhere. I attended Sunday school while they were in their church services. I looked forward to the lessons, stories, and singing the songs.

Grandma's days began in the kitchen seeing that everyone had breakfast. Grandpa had the same thing every day. Porridge, as he called it, and a soft boiled egg which sat in a little egg cup so he could "whack" it with his knife and eat each half with a spoon. Since Kellogg's hadn't invented cereal (corn flakes) yet, we all pretty much ate the same things, oatmeal, toast (maybe with cinnamon & sugar), some occasional pancakes, milk, hot chocolate or tea & coffee for the "grown-ups".

Next, she would be planning the day's cooking & baking so the bread or rolls would have time to rise. It was a rare day she didn't bake something. She baked all our bread, biscuits, and cinnamon rolls. She made wild blackberry cobblers and jams, apple pies, thick freshly made noodles and dumplings to go with the chicken or rabbit, side dishes like creamed fresh shelled peas and new potatoes and so much more.

When she wasn't cooking, there was general cleaning, water to heat for laundry, the clothes to be hopefully hung outside on sunny days, and on the rainy days, they hung around the kitchen on wooden drying racks. Later, she ironed them with flat irons heated on the wood cook stove. I can still see the beads of sweat on her brow as she stood next to that hot stove exchanging the irons back and forth.

And, as if that weren't enough, there was sewing, mending and even darning to be done. At least she could sit down awhile while she worked on them. I don't know one person these days who would bother to turn shirt collars, darn socks or make children's coats out of discarded adult coats. Those things just get tossed out now or perhaps donated to a place like Goodwill.

The only time I can remember her doing something not work related happened when they went to church or when she occasionally sat down at the piano and played a few hymns. She always said something to the effect that the Devil put idle hands to work for him.

But overall, the kitchen remained totally her domain. We could set the table or dry some dishes with those "former flour sacks" which she transformed into soft dish towels, maybe snap some beans, shell some peas or peel some potatoes, but that was about it. After all, it WAS Grandma's Kitchen!

* * *

"The War Years"

The year: 1942. World War II continued to escalate. No one's life was unaffected by it in some way, be it school children or adults. Gasoline and many other commodities were rationed or simply not available at any price. People sought out others with whom they could trade or even sell their coupons.

After buying and bartering all they could, the only way of stretching gas allotments, for example, meant walking, riding the bus, sharing rides and even going so far as to turn off the engine to coast down hills to save a tiny bit.

I remember my mother doing this one day while my aunt rode with us in the car. Her husband, my father's brother served in the army as well, and they both laughed as they coasted down a hill. Perhaps I felt fear, or for whatever reason at the time, I didn't think it a bit funny, and told them so. They just laughed all the harder. I guess I was just too young to see the "adult" humor in the situation.

Also, during that time period, everyone saved every dollar or dime they could to buy U.S. War Bonds to "help the war effort." Even children saved their coins to purchase savings stamps, paste them into booklets, and then turn them in for "war" bonds when they were full.

Posters were everywhere with a stern looking "Uncle Sam" pointing his finger and saying, "Uncle Sam Wants You!" The war came up as a continuous topic of conversation. Recycling, an everyday thing, involved even saving the tinfoil from gum and candy wrappers. Patriotism wasn't just a word, it was a way of life then!

When President Roosevelt addressed the nation on the radio, everyone sat close by, leaning forward, listening intently, waiting to hear the latest news. Even the children sat quietly. The broadcasts were usually clear, but sometimes, the static and crackling noises threatened to drown out his voice. Everyone concentrated even harder, not wanting to miss a word. The other way we learned anything at that time came through the movies when they played those grainy black & white Movietone newsreels. Sometimes they frightened you and other times they made you proud! I can still remember the theme music they played as they came on the screen.

My father served in the U. S. Army, stationed at Camp Fannin, Texas, near the town of Tyler. My understanding was he was a Staff Sargent and trained troops there. He wrote a few post cards to me, mostly asking why I didn't write to him more often. Too busy being a child, I guess. He was not a demonstrative man, nor was he mean, but we'd not been really close.

My mother went to work for Safeway, basically taking over his job as a butcher there. I still have the newspaper article, now yellow and brittle, complete with her picture behind the meat counter, headlined "First Lady Butcher" in North Bend, Oregon. I guess you could call her the local "Rosie the Riveter" in the butcher shop!

My best memory, though involves Grandma's kitchen. A wonderful cook, keeping that big, cast iron wood stove in constant use. My memories of her are many.

One of my favorite recollections will always be of walking in after school and smelling that aroma of freshly baked bread; the loaves still cooling on the counter covered by those clean flour sacks that had been recycled and now served as dish towels.

Grandma would sometimes tear a portion off one end of a loaf when they were still too warm to slice, place a chunk of real butter on it, and while it melted, place a small bowl of real maple syrup in front of me to dip it in. What a wonderful treat that was! Perhaps that was her way of giving me hugs!

And yes, I even remember all those clattering sounds that came from her cooking in those iron skillets on that iron cook stove, and the physical and emotional warmth and aroma of that room that emanated both from the heat of the stove and from all the good things she cooked and served there.

Even the war seemed a little farther away when you were in grandma's kitchen.

* * *

"And 'Little' Grandma, Too. . ."

I know least of all about Great Grandma McCarty, another person living in the same house during the time period when Mother and I lived with her parents. She was Grandma Tewsley's mother, and since there were two Grandmas in the household, we delineated between the two by calling her "Little Grandma".

She was born Mary Ellen Cunning and was born in Coshocton, Ohio. She married George Brock Haw. According to the birth certificate for Grandma Tewsley, he was born near Point Hope, Ontario, and was 31 at the time of her birth. She was 25. That would make her date of birth sometime in 1858. According to that same birth record, she was the third child born to them and the only one living. They lived in Ipswich, South Dakota at the time of her birth.

She was small in stature compared to Grandma Tewsley, who although small herself was only deemed larger by comparing the two of them. In retrospect, she seemed to be fairly frail as she always used a cane, but then she had to be around 84 or a bit more having been born in 1858. In remembering her, I visualize her sitting on the couch in the living room. She must have done other things, but to my child's mind it seems she sat there most of the time.

She tatted, crocheted, and did embroidery. No idle hands here, either. Sometimes as I passed through she would ask me to thread a needle for her. I asked her one day why she asked me to thread them for her, and she told me it was because I could see so much better than she and it made it difficult for her to thread them. I really didn't mind and never asked again. She tried to teach me to tat, but at that age it seemed a whole lot of work for the little bit of (beautiful) edging you turned out. Much more fun to go out and play or to draw things.

My only other real memory of her is of playing a game called "Birds in the Bush". I'd sit on the couch beside her and we'd both have an allotment of marbles. We'd hold some in our hands and shake them and the other person would guess how many. If you were right, you got the marbles. She usually won, but it was something to do on those rainy days. I enjoyed spending the time with her.

I don't know when she became widowed or divorced from George Haw, but I knew her as Grandma McCarty (little grandma). When she was widowed from Mr. McCarty, Grandma T. brought her out to Oregon to live with them. My mother later said that turned out to be a mistake, as she had left behind everyone she knew for so many years, and had no real way of making new friends out here. Only grandpa drove a car and she would have been too frail to take the bus anywhere, especially alone. So Sunday morning church was really her only outing. No senior centers or things of that sort then.

She passed away sometime during the six months I spent in Texas in 1945, at the age of 88. When I came back, she "just wasn't there anymore".

* * *

"Then There Was Grandpa"

He was born October 27, 1869 in Canada. There isn't a city listed in the little information I have for him. His name was John Henry Tewsley and he was a wheat farmer. In his later years, in the early 1940's and beyond, when my memories of him begin, he was a builder, a house painter and what you might call a "horse trader" of sorts. He bought, sold and traded to get what they needed beyond what he worked for. He seemed to do well at it. He had a knack for making ridiculous offers and having people agree to take them or trade with him in some way. Perhaps it was his education? He was well spoken, and had the most beautiful penmanship I have ever seen for a man, and perhaps even a woman. Even as a child, I remember watching him as he wrote something, and seeing it made me want to write better.

On December 16, 1903, he married Grandma. Her maiden name, according to her birth certificate was Laura Bell Haw. He would have been 34 at the time and she would have been only 20. Born in Ipswich, North Dakota, USA, on July 27, 1883, made her 14 years his junior. Her birth certificate indicates her mother and father were both living in Ipswich at that time. It also shows her mother as having been born in Sochocton, Ohio and her father's birthplace as "near" Port Hope, Ontario, and lists his occupation as a farmer. I can only guess the family migrated to Canada before she met grandpa, since her father was from there originally.

She became a farmer's wife and bore him seven children. All were born in Yorkton, Saskatchewan. My mother was number five of the seven.

Life was certainly much harder for everyone in those times, but unless you were of genteel birth, I believe it was much harder for women like my grandmother. She only got to go through the fourth grade in regular school as she was required to stay home and help her mother care for her two younger sisters. She was baking the family bread at age ten. None of that stopped her from doing all she could to educate herself at home, however, and she spoke and wrote as if she had gone much farther in school.

I have no doubt Grandpa was a hard worker, but when their work day ended, the men of that era sat and waited for their dinner to be served and rested afterward while the women washed dishes and finished any other chores needing to be done before bedtime.

They seemingly did fairly well with their farming. All the old pictures show them and their children well dressed, and they sent the older girls for piano lessons and one on to nursing school and another to secretarial school. Unfortunately, tragedy struck their home in 1927 when there was a strep throat epidemic. The oldest daughter came home from nursing school to help care for the family when the youngest daughter died at age seven, and she followed her in death ten days later. She was only 20 and would have graduated from nursing school in three months. Both girls were ill only 48 hours.

It seems that financially things began to go the wrong direction not too long after that. Perhaps they may have been affected by the stock market crash even though they were in Canada at that time, or perhaps there was a drought or some other quirk of nature. My understanding is they lost the farm or farms. Mother had mentioned at one point they lived at one place in summer and one in winter. I have found no further information or pictures in support of that, but she talked about all the extra work and cooking grandma had to do to feed the threshers and keep everything going smoothly at harvest time. She also mentioned grandma's sister sending her two children out there in the summers for her to feed and care for. My mother resented that she was given and accepted the extra work while the aunt relaxed in town.

Perhaps that was because she had always cared for the sisters when she had to stay home from school. Another interesting thing on her birth certificate was the fact that although she was listed as the third child, she was listed as the only one living. One can only wonder whether the first two were stillborn or died later, and whether they were boys or girls. The two sisters she did end up with were 6 and 10 years younger than her. Were there possibly others in between that also didn't survive?

Most of the remaining family migrated to the US in 1931, ending up in Empire, Oregon. If it ever was an actual town, it was slowly absorbed by the two nearby towns Marshfield and North Bend. Marshfield later was renamed Coos Bay. The high school is still called Marshfield.

My mother was 16 at the time. She didn't go on to finish high school or other schooling down here as the older girls had done in Canada. Her younger brother, Gordon, was about five and her older sister, Elsie, 20. The other sister, Genevieve, 26 by that time, had married and stayed in Canada. Their older brother had gone in the service. He was later killed in a mining accident in Canada. He had married and left a wife and young son.

Times were extremely tough! They lived in an old store front trying to make it as much like a home as possible. One of their staples for food was the clams they dug at low tide. Mother once said they had clams fixed every way possible, plus they canned the extra ones. She said it was a wonder she could even look at a clam today let alone eat one!

Grandma and Grandpa did find work in a logging camp where they stayed all week and came home on the weekends. Grandma was the chief cook but Grandpa, her helper, also did handyman work as needed. They stayed at the camp all week and came home on weekends bringing with them the week's leftover food. At that time, the girls were old enough to take care of themselves and the younger brother during the week.

I don't know the exact time or circumstances, whether it was bought, traded or possibly even given to them, but somehow Grandpa acquired an old house in Empire, tore it down board by board, fashioned or found himself a trailer of some sort and hauled it all to a lot on Newmark Street in North Bend and built them another house. Indeed, quite the handyman! This is the house where mother and I later lived with them for almost three years.

When you think about his age, he would have been 62 when they migrated from Canada, and probably in his later 60's when he finished building that house. He was never one to have idle hands either. There were chickens and rabbits to feed or butcher and gardens to tend. He found other houses in need of repair to buy and sell. When mother wasn't working at Safeway, she would sometimes help him with painting or wall papering and make a few extra dollars herself or perhaps help pay our room and board. Under his tutoring, she became quite the expert paper hanger and he was happy to turn over as much of it to her as he could. He much preferred to be painting or doing the carpentry work.

He would have been about 67 when I was born and so in his early 70's with snow white hair when I have any real recollection of him. Not a mean man, but he was stern and brooked no extra noise or nonsense. I had no fear of him, but it didn't occur to me not to do what he said either. Children were to be seen and not heard, so it seemed to me there was often some "shushing" going on. Occasionally, though, he played a game of Dominoes or Rummy. Just don't take too long to play or the fingers would start drumming on the table impatiently.

I remember taking a family trip to or from where I don't know or perhaps it was our destination, but we stopped at Belknap Hot Springs and went swimming. I remember being so surprised to see him in an old black wool bathing suit and swimming kind of crab like, or so it seemed to me, back and forth across the pool. Grandpa could swim? I had also never seen him any way but fully dressed.

I was told he got his driver's license back when you could send a quarter in to the state and be registered. I can believe he never took a driving lesson and as I got older I was even more amazed. He would roll his window down about an inch or so and then stick his fingers out to signal he was going to turn. Near as I could tell, you had to guess whether it was left or right!

I rode in the back seat on Sunday mornings when they took me to Sunday school while they attended church services. It always seemed to me he never looked left or right, just straight ahead. He'd back that big black sedan out of the garage looking straight ahead down past the side of the house and then turn left before he could go straight ahead. I can remember him scraping the side of the house once and backing over a slight bank at the turn a couple of times, then putting it in forward gear and revving the engine till it came back over the bank. As you might imagine, he had trouble keeping brakes and clutches in his cars.

I remember being embarrassed as a teenager when a group laughed at how a car was parked downtown. It should have been parallel parked, but instead the nose was in and the back was still partially in the street. I didn't let on it was Grandpa's car!

I can't verify whether true or not, but it was suggested he was from Scottish ancestry. I do know he loved to tell Scottish jokes and had the brogue down perfect. He must have had a great memory as he took great pride in never telling the same joke to the same person twice.

All in all, an honest, intelligent, hard working individual. One of those "old fashioned" people whose word was their bond and a handshake closed the deal!